Country Ways

in Sussex and Surrey

Other titles in this series:
Country Ways in Kent
Country Ways in Hampshire and Dorset

Country Ways

in Sussex and Surrey

ANTHONY HOWARD

Countryside Books/TVS

First Published 1986
© Text Anthony Howard 1986

Countryside Books
3 Catherine Road,
Newbury, Berkshire.

ISBN 0 905392 68 X

Front Cover Photograph: Robin Fletcher
Back Cover Photograph: Derek Budd

Photographs by Derek Budd, Tony Nutley and Tim Sharman

Produced through MRM (Print Consultants) Ltd, Reading
Typeset by Acorn Bookwork, Salisbury
Printed in England by Borcombe Printers, Romsey

CONTENTS

1   Ashdown Forest   11

2   The South Downs   20

3   Selsey   31

4   Rye   39

5   Balcombe   48

6   Frensham Ponds   55

7   Pevensey Levels   68

INTRODUCTION

Tommy Beeton's favourite day out was to go ferreting with his friends. His skill at catching rabbits in the little loose nets which he pegged firmly over each burrow was unchallenged. And his patience while digging out a ferret which had killed a rabbit in an underground cul-de-sac and had settled down for a feast and a sleep, was complete. He used an ancient long-bladed pointed spade, and hummed while he dug with effortless rhythm. He ploughed geometrically straight furrows with horses or with the iron-wheeled Fordson Major tractor. And he could talk with great accuracy about approaching weather – judging it by the direction in which the mice in the hedges were digging their holes. He had genuine wisdom about the cycle of life and death and the countryside, handed down through generations of peasant workers. Yet he could neither read nor write.

If Tommy was alive, he would have been able to make a colourful contribution to *Country Ways*. People like him still exist in the depths of the English countryside and, although their worth and wisdom have sometimes been diluted by the doubtful benefits of progress, it is still valuable and fascinating to record their thoughts before their way of life dies with them.

At first sight Surrey and Sussex are unlikely counties to find much of the old world still in existence. The stockbroker belt has left its own indelible mark on the area, and its own unmistakable accents. Brighton and Eastbourne, Guildford and Godalming, Haywards Heath and Hastings have become dormitories for London or rest homes for the retired. But pockets of resistance remain, where original country voices can still be heard and country habits observed. In some ways the countryside character of these suburban counties is the strongest of all. If it has managed to survive thus far against the invasion of people with city instincts it must be very durable indeed.

The tranquillity of Frensham Ponds is less than an hour away from the hustle and bustle of London.

A woodmouse feeding on the seeds of rosebay willow herb in Ashdown Forest.

Ashdown Forest at sunrise.

ASHDOWN FOREST

ASHDOWN Forest is in the middle of Sussex and is surrounded by East Grinstead, Crowborough, Haywards Heath and Crawley. It is also Winnie-the-Pooh country and it takes A. A. Milne to describe it adequately. 'By the time it came to the edge of the Forest the stream had grown up, so that it was almost a river and, being grown up, it did not run and jump and sparkle along as it used to do when it was younger, but moved more slowly. For it knew now where it was going and it said to itself – "There is no hurry. We shall get there some day". But all the little streams higher up in the Forest went this way and that, quickly, eagerly, having so much to find out before it was too late.'

Ashdown Forest was originally created as a Royal hunting-ground. Its 14,000 acres of wooded heathland are ablaze, in season, with heather, gorse and bracken. The land rises to 700 feet at Beacon Hill and three rivers – the Medway, the Ouse and the East Rother – emerge from its sterile and sandy soil. To improve the stag-hunting, many trees were cut down. Edward II had a hunting lodge built at Nutley and Edward III made a gift of the area to his son, John of Gaunt, the Duke of Lancaster. Because of this the Forest used to be known as Lancaster Great Park. During the reign of Charles II the region passed into the hands of the Earls of Dorset. One of them started to enclose some of the land. In the courts judgement was made against the Earl, and this ruling established common rights for over 6,000 acres. The right to graze animals and to cut wood and bracken still exists, but it is seldom exercised in an area which is almost exclusively middle and upper class.

In the twentieth century the most notorious event in the Ashdown Forest area was the discovery in 1912 at the village of Piltdown by the geologist Charles Dawson of the skull fragments of what everyone accepted as a prehistoric man. Much later it was proved scientifically not to be so, and Dawson was discredited after having led the scientific world to believe that a major anthropological find had been made. Unlike many reputable scientists Dawson's fame lives on in the form of a pub with a grim sign outside showing The Piltdown Man.

Although it stands in the middle of the stockbroker belt there is still a wealth of plants, trees and wildlife in the Forest, including many, timid deer. Some village names like Buckhurst and Hartfield, where A. A. Milne lived and wrote the Pooh stories, echo the distant stag-hunting days. And places like Wren's Warren and Crowborough Warren recall the times when there was a huge rabbit population.

11

Local accents have largely disappeared, but Ashdown Forest still retains much tranquillity and dignity. Some genuine country people have managed to hang on in spite of the rocketing prices of local property. But the constant stream of heavy and fast-moving traffic along the unfenced roads is now a hazard for deer, sheep and horses.

AT Wych Cross Margaret Wilcock's herd of fine white goats are hardly typical of the livestock in the area. But they are all in a day's work for vet, Christine Howe from Uckfield, whose practice includes the whole of Ashdown Forest. She pays regular visits to the small farm and her firm and sensitive hands explore the limbs of the goats for the causes of their aches and pains. But she certainly would not call herself a goat specialist.

'We're a very mixed practice. We do everything from aquariums to rabbits to goats. I myself do nearly all cattle work – dairy cows most of the time – and also quite a lot of horses. It's a knack I suppose. You learn how to deal with these big animals. If you didn't you'd soon be out of business. I was brought up with cattle and with horses all my life, and you just get a way of dealing with them. Occasionally you get stroppy ones that you have to sedate or to use other methods. But then, it's not just the big ones. Even rabbits can be a problem. They've got very good claws!'

Margaret brings a kid with a lame leg into the small barn, where chickens peck at the dust and chirpy sparrows fly in and out. The young goat is clearly in pain and Christine examines it tenderly. Whatever the cause, time, as so often is the case, will be the cure. In addition a pain-killing injection is carefully squeezed into the flesh of the hind leg. All seems well as Christine hurries away to her next appointment. 'This part of the world has a real hold on me. There's an awful lot of different types of landscape. There's the Forest itself and then, nearby, there's the downs, the coastline, the woods. There's everything here. There are people from all walks of life. You've got everything from the country farmer to the stockbroker to the millionaire. If I'm honest my one dislike of the area is that there are too many people.'

IRON has been made in Ashdown Forest since Roman times and the streams still carry signs of the iron deposits – rusty, orange sludge beside the clear water. Charcoal-burners used the forest trees for their blast-furnaces and the local people had to try to protect as much of the woodland as they could. In the early autumn the birds of the forest are elusive and strangely silent – not because of the lack of trees, but because they are too busy moulting or feeding up for long migrations to sing and quarrel as they did back in the summer. However, there is still a captive audience of every kind of feathered creature at Sheffield Park on the edge of Ashdown Forest. There, Don Harrison and his wife have dedicated their lives to rescue and care for injured and unwanted birds of every colour of the rainbow. There are parrots and canaries, seagulls and herons, owls and hawks all living together in noisy harmony.

'Our busiest time of the year is normally December, January and February when there are gales. Then we get vast numbers of oiled sea birds, which are always a great problem to us. Some of them are terribly injured, but we don't take the decision to put any bird down unless it is suffering. If it can enjoy its life in any form – even if it has only one wing and can still enjoy itself – we do not end its life. We let it live.'

There is a smart bird hospital at Wingshaven – the name of the Harrison's home. Here they carry out every kind of delicate operation, and many of their former patients are still with them. A large parrot's head peeps out of an old beer barrel with a hole cut in the side. It stays so still and silent that you think it must be made of plastic or pottery. Then it blinks and the spell is broken. Nearby small birds hop and flutter round a big cage, and owls sit and stare from the back of a dark shed. On a pond with a fountain, water birds and waders swim and feed. 'In the summer months we get a vast range of birds here. We get brought lots of garden birds because of people using insecticides or pesticides heavily on their borders or in their fruit trees. Of the owls that come our way I would think that, on the whole, we save over eighty percent. Probably about five or six percent die. There are another four or five percent, which we have to put down. Roughly ten percent are fit for partial rehabilitation, and we find homes for those or keep them here ourselves for educational purposes. So it's between 70–80% that go back to the wild.'

But inevitably it is the exotic birds which catch the eye. The blues and greens and reds and yellows of the macaws and parrots and smaller tropical birds shine like torches in the dull, winter landscape. 'I think the main reason that we come by so many of these is the noise they make. It's a really big problem. People buy them and don't realise what they're in for. Neighbours complain about the amount of noise that a cockatoo will make. It's much noisier than a dog for instance. And then there are problems indoors, because, if you have a parrot or a macaw in the house, he will soon destroy a lot of his surroundings. And it isn't fair to keep him shut up in his cage. And then there are people going overseas and so on. They bring their birds here until they come back, or they bring them for their safety. We've just lost one macaw and she was well over a hundred years old. That's quite unusual, but most of them live fifty, sixty, seventy or eighty years. People don't realise what they're taking on when they get a bird. It's far more trouble than a dog or cat.'

It is a non-stop job for the Harrisons at Wingshaven. They are on duty every day of the week and every week of the year. There is no financial reward, but there are other valuable results. 'We get a great many young children who bring in birds, and we pay special attention to them. Because, when the child comes back in two or three weeks and sees the bird outside in the aviary or watches us release it back into the wild, you've got a conservationist for life.'

And Don Harrison turns away and walks up a narrow path towards the water, to make sure that there is enough food for his noisy waders and sea-birds, while the eyes of owls and macaws follow him without curiosity.

RIDING is predictably popular in Ashdown Forest and horses are everywhere. Sian Williams from Cackle Lane, Nutley keeps four of her own in a pleasant meadow behind her home. But her business is to make and repair harness and horse-rugs for the riders of the Forest.

'I've always worked with horses. I've always loved them and anything to do with them. I don't remember actually starting with horses, but I must have done sometime. There are between three and five hundred being ridden on the Forest and I get a lot of their custom. So it keeps me out of mischief. The only difficulty is the roads. Roads and horses do not mix, which is why I'm so glad we have the Forest. Horses can be very unpredictable on the roads. It only takes a little white bag or something to frighten them. People don't seem to realise just how quickly a horse can move across a road if it's scared, though I think car drivers are just beginning to get the message.'

Sian's small workshop is spick and span. Everything is in its place and, as she bends over her work, the sun shines in across the field, where her horses are grazing. Her long, supple fingers fight the leather, and the sewing machine hums and protests. The clean smell of harness dominates the house. 'It's hard work, especially the heavier pieces of harness. It can be very tough. And, in general, it's interesting too. I also try to do different things to give myself variety. I even mend handbags and make leather skirts, and I've done repairs to motorbike leathers and altered them. When I'm looking at a bridle for quality I look to see if it has been edged properly. That means that it's not sharp on your hands and it's not sharp on your horse, and that the edges are polished nicely and good-fitting. There's quite a lot to making bridles. You've got to cut the leather first and edge it. Then you've got to stamp your holes — however many to the inch you're going to put for your stitching. Next there's the polishing. I'm sometimes sad that people can't tell the difference between a well-made bridle and one that isn't so good. If they'd look carefully they'd see the difference. But they don't seem to bother sometimes.'

Everything about Sian's life seems perfect — even her hobby, which is playing the harp. 'My parents went out to buy me a rocking-horse for Christmas. In one of the junk shops they visited my mother found this harp, and she bought it as a surprise for my father. And he's restored it. It's a very old harp and a lovely instrument.' As the strong fingers caress the taut strings, the soft music drifts through the window and becomes part of the magic of Ashdown Forest.

EVEN on the murkiest winter day there is work for Paul and Marion Wilcock on their unique farm at Wych Cross. Their enterprise is devoted to keeping alive rare breeds of farm animals and poultry — the sort of creatures that were a common sight on peasant farms in the Middle Ages. As the rain drips from the eaves, Paul and Marion feed and muck out and care for groups of animals, which most people will never have seen before. 'We used to live down at the other side of the Forest. But we wanted more land for the animals. We were collecting more than we could keep, and

Paul Wilcock trimming the feet of a Soay sheep at the Rare Breeds Farm at Wych Cross.

we like the area very much. It's hard. The ground isn't particularly good, so we get a very sparse grass growth, so that the old breeds off the mountains don't grow fat. They stay in their natural form, as they were in the old days.'

Paul starts work trimming the feet of a pen of Wensleydale sheep – large, strong, lank-haired creatures and a struggle to get hold of in the wet conditions. 'They come from Yorkshire. They're famous for their great, long coats, which are very silky. They were bred over the centuries for the length and the particular quality of their fleeces. They're now very low in numbers, I'm afraid. They have about 180% lambing rate and they are used for crossing to increase fertility. But, above all, they are bred for the fleece. It grows a millimetre a day, which means that by the end of a year you've got over a foot of wool on most ewes, and a shearling could have eighteen inches of fleece on it.'

Meanwhile, Marion is on the other side of the farm trying to get to grips with some agile, little brown sheep with curly horns and mischievous faces. 'These are rather lovely. They're the smallest of all the British breeds. They're fell sheep, which means that they're almost wild. So they're difficult to handle. The thing that most

15

people don't realise about them is that they don't have a fleece which you can shear like you normally do. You actually pluck the wool out. They've also discovered that they're so light on their feet that they are suitable for grazing on reclaimed land. So they've been using them in Cornwall, where they're reclaiming the old china clay pits.'

In a well-fenced meadow stand three Old Gloucestershire cattle, brownish black in colour with a narrow white line running along the middle of their backs to the top of their tails. There is some distant flavour of Red Indians in their war-paint about them, with their identical and symmetrical markings. 'These very nearly became extinct. They lost favour to the Friesians. Now the only ones that are kept alive are looked after by enthusiasts like us. There's also one commercial herd, which is producing milk specially for Double Gloucester cheese, which was their original purpose in life.'

The neighbours of the Gloucester cattle are some pure white cows, whose shining coats are only slightly marked by the muddy conditions. 'The British Whites are the

Marion Wilcock with a proud mother and baby, just two of the animals at this unusual farm in the heart of Ashdown Forest.

16

big success story of the rare breeds. In 1980 there were something like 285 of them left. Now there are well over 400 pure registered British Whites. They're mainly used for crossing with dairy breeds to produce beef cows. It's a sad fact that it's not until you have nearly lost your breed that you realise that it has got qualities which haven't previously been appreciated. And then sometimes it's too late.'

Throughout the Wilcock's holding, unusual chickens, doves, bantams and turkeys stroll freely among the fenced animals. Round the end of a fine, newly-thatched barn comes a vast turkey. Its head comes up to Paul's waist. 'These big, bronze turkeys are very special to me. We're going to breed them. They're not going to be on anybody's table for Christmas. But they would be a superb turkey to eat. They would have a much more gamey, much stronger meat than ordinary commercial turkeys.'

In an untypical pile of untidy straw and mud at the bottom of the hill on which the farm stands, small, turned-up noses grunt and beady, black eyes stare. As Marion brings their food, tiny black pigs bundle out of the straw and snort and fight over the meal. 'All our pigs are hardy and particularly these little, black Vietnamese pot-bellied ones. They are identical to the pigs they have running around in the yards behind shacks in the Far East. We decided that as they're so strong, we would try the traditional way of housing them in old straw-houses. So the other day we made them what we thought was a very beautiful bale-house. I'm afraid that we didn't get it quite right because, when we came down the next morning, there was just this big heap of straw with the little pigs with their heads sticking out the top, and all you could see was their little eyes. But they were quite happy, although it was just as well that there were no big, bad wolves about.' That's one of the few animals you cannot find in this extraordinary Noah's Ark in the heart of Ashdown Forest just an hour from Central London.

AT Fords Green in the middle of the Forest you are likely as not to find Fred Kirby chopping and splitting wood behind his cottage. He is a small, eager man in his seventies and one of the real Ashdown Forest old-timers. He is called the wood or manor reeve and his job is to look after and to control the cutting of heather and wood, and the digging of stone. Above all, he loves the area and its trees and views. 'The autumn is my favourite time, when the trees are all changing colour and the heather's out. I like it especially then 'cos I'm a beekeeper, you see, and the bees get a lot of honey from the heather. So that's one of the main reasons for liking the autumn. I can remember it when we were children. There wasn't the amount of people then, and you could walk about easy. But today, every little nook and corner there's a car parked in or somebody courtin' or somethin' like that, you see.'

The quiet voice has lost none of its local colour because of the invasion of city folk and, as so often with genuine countrymen, the enthusiasm of youth remains. Fred loves to go out walking in his beloved beech woods in all weathers to sniff the air and to see what is stirring. 'It does get a bit harsh at times, if you get a bad winter. This

Ashdown Forest was originally created as a royal hunting ground, and covers 14,000 acres of wooded heathland.

used to be a home for the Forest commoners, you know. Commoners have certain rights and can go out onto the Forest and cut birch, willow or elder and things like that. But today it's overspill from London practically all the time, you see. One time, you'd see a commoner going out getting his firewood for lighting the fire, and, perhaps, his wife 'anging out the washin' on a line in the Forest. But you don't see that today.'

When he is off in the woodland Fred always carries with him his gnarled and trusty swordstick, a formidable weapon which has been handed down through generations of his family. 'It's a three-purpose stick. When you're going through the breaks, if they're wet, you can poke 'em to one side with it. Then sometimes I've had a dog come at me – once a big alsation – and it's just the thing for parrying them off, you see. And then, if a man comes after you – or, like in my grandad's day, a highwayman – you've got the sword as a final defence. The old original rangers used to have these sticks. That was the only weapon they were allowed to carry, you see.'

18

Even the privileged commoners are forbidden to cut down the kings of the Forest – the majestic oaks and beeches, which still have pride of place across the area. 'There's a Preservation Order on the trees of the Forest nowadays, so people can't come in and chop them down, even if they're willing to pay. I don't think there's any danger of these great trees dying out round 'ere, because they're so good at re-seeding theirselves. When the beech-nuts or acorns drop, it's amazin' how far the squirrels or pigeons carry them away before they let 'em fall. Then they germinate. And that's how you get a beech tree or an oak coming up where there's never been a tree before.'

SOMETIMES Fred Kirby's walks take him up to the top of the Forest, where there are spacious views and tranquillity. And it was here that Winnie the Pooh and Christopher Robin, with a little help from A. A. Milne, created some of their special magic. 'By and by they came to an enchanted place on the very top of the Forest called Galleon's Lap, which is sixty-something trees in a circle; and Christopher Robin knew that it was enchanted, because nobody had ever been able to count whether it was sixty-three or sixty-four – not even when he tied a piece of string round each tree after he had counted it.

'Being enchanted, its floor was not like the floor of the Forest, gorse and bracken and heather, but close-set grass, quiet and smooth and green. It was the only place in the Forest where you could sit down carelessly, without getting up again almost at once and looking for somewhere else. Sitting there they could see the whole world spread out until it reached the sky, and whatever there was all the world over was with them in Galleon's Lap.'

THE SOUTH DOWNS

THE South Downs stand as a strong and beautiful bastion along the centre of the English Channel coast. Some of the finest walks in the world are here; some of the most dramatic views; some of the best pubs; some of the most successful farmers. Beloved by artists and poets, they were described by Kipling as 'these blunt, bow-headed, whale-backed Downs'. And Mrs Marriott Watson wrote:

> 'Broad and bare to the skies
> The great Downs country lies,
> Green in the glance of the sun,
> Fresh with the keen, salt air;
> Screaming, the gulls rise from the fresh-turned mould
> Where the round bosom of the wind-swept fold
> Slopes to the valley fair.'

Seen from the sea on a summer's day the whiteness of the chalk is dazzling. And the symmetry of the Seven Sisters, just to the east of Seaford, makes them look as though they have been perfectly designed by an artistic computer.

The South Downs rise at Pevensey and run past Chichester. From Beachy Head and on into West Sussex the main block of the Downland extends for fifty-three miles, the first sixteen of which hug the sea in a continuous white cliff to Brighton. They then leave the coast and head inland. Four rivers cut their way through the chalk — the Cuckmere, The Ouse, the Arun and the Lavant. Each has its own particular charm and character, and each is well worth exploring in its own right.

Certainly the people of the Downland area are fiercely loyal to the region, and echo in their praises the words of the naturalist, Gilbert White. 'Though I have now travelled the Sussex Downs upwards of thirty years, yet I still investigate that chain of majestic mountains with fresh admiration year by year, and I think I see new beauties in it every time I traverse it.'

THE South Downs have given their name to a special breed of sheep, much favoured on these chalky slopes in the past, but few and far between today. Jack Coleman from Ringmer is one of the last shepherds with a pedigree flock of South

Jack Coleman from Ringmer is one of the last shepherds with a pedigree flock of South Down sheep.

Downs, and he and his faithful old dog, Quick, watch over them night and day. Jack is not so fast on his feet as once he was, but he is still a wiry, old man with good eyes and quick hands, and he can upend a big ewe to give her feet the once-over with the best of them.

'There's two little old cottages side by side just south of Ringmer. I was born in the top one and I live in the bottom one. That's as far as I've got in my life. I don't know any other life. It's all the life I've had. My father was a shepherd and when I was about two years old I used to go out working with him. Whether I was a help or hindrance I don't know. We used to drive the sheep from here to the sheep sales at Lewes. We'd go right up over the Downs and drive them through to the town. That was when I was five years old. We used to walk there and walk back. I was tired out by the time I got home on those days. Then I left school at fourteen. I left one Friday night, and started shepherding Saturday morning for ten shillings a week.'

And there is a tinge of regret in the old voice and sadness in the eyes. 'We'd have several flocks of sheep on the hills in them days, and we used to put bells on them in the winter-time. Then we knew where the next shepherd's sheep were grazing, so we didn't get mixed up. If you got a dense fog, which happens a lot up here, you couldn't see nothin'. But you could hear these bells, and you knew you'd got to keep away from them, and get back to your own boundary a bit.'

Jack heads back home for tea in his little cottage at the foot of the steep hill. He looks out one more time across the valley, as if he is making sure that it is still imprinted clearly on his mind and his memory. 'I think I'm the last of the South Downs shepherds. But it's sad, cause these hills were covered in South Down sheep and nothing else up here – no fences, no cattle, just sheep. But they've gone now.' And the small figure disappears down the hill along a path, which he must have trodden ten thousand times.

BOB Copper's family can be traced back for generations as farm workers in Rottingdean. Bob has kept treasured books of the old Sussex and Downland songs which go back to his great-grandfather. Today, the family takes pride in keeping these songs alive. They sing unaccompanied and with great harmony in pubs and clubs along the South Downs. But for real pleasure Bob likes to stride out across the hills in search of fresh air and long, relaxing views.

'I've always loved these old hills and it goes back to my father and my grandfather. They worked on 'em. My father was a shepherd boy from the age of eleven, and my grand-dad could beat that. He was a shepherd boy at the age of nine. There were 250,000 sheep between Beachy Head and Steyning – just that section of the Downs – and they were all grazed on the hills. They called it sheep-run or sheep-turf and that's why so many of these old songs that we sing are shepherds' songs, you see.'

They make a handsome family group as they stand in front of a roaring log fire surrounded by old horse brasses and sing the ancient family songs to a group of drinkers and their dogs. It is old-fashioned entertainment, but seems to hold the attention of the listeners. Many a hard, lined face softens as the words recall days long forgotten. 'My earliest memories are when I went home from school at lunch-time. Very often Mum would say "There's the dinner. Take it up to your Dad". I'd say, "Where is he, Mum". "Oh, he's up Socks" or "He's up Honeysocks". I had to know where all the different fields were and what their names were, because I had to get back home quickly, and have my own dinner in time to go back to school at half-past one.'

Bob Copper's kind, florid face lights up when he speaks of his beloved South Downs. Generations have handed down to him this sense of belonging to the place. And he feels true emotion for it. 'Open Downs and an open sky, the old skylarks and corn buntings singing away up there. It's truly lovely. There's such a feeling of freedom around the Downs. You've got terrific views, and the landscapes are marvellous. But the sky-scapes are even better.' And, as he speaks, the white clouds race across the broad, blue sky and, out at sea, the freshening wind creates its own white patches on the water.

GRAHAM Baker from Glynde, near Lewes, is a keen coarse fisherman. He sits for hours at a time by the canal across the meadow from his home. The swans glide by and, now and again, he has a bite and pulls a fish from the black water. He is a short, strong, dark man with burn marks on his arms for, by profession, he is a skilled and talented blacksmith and farrier. But his great love is for the South Downs and he is devoted to the area.

'I've had five moves in my life, but I've never been out of sight of this part of the Downs. I've always wanted to live within viewing distance of 'em. Personally I think it's one of the prettiest places there is around. It's got its own character. You've got places in Wales and that – and they're all different. But, for me, this has got to be about the best. It's in my blood, I suppose.'

Framing the huge door of Graham's smithy is a giant wooden horseshoe. It is a work of art and, although it is standing the wrong way up, it does not seem to have brought bad luck with it. 'It was fitted there by the workmen on the estate. Passers-by are always stopping to look at it. It must be unique, and I don't think there can be another forge like this one. The majority of the work I do is cold shoe forging, and I go virtually all over the place. It's much easier for me to go to the horses and to do eight or nine in one place, than what it is for them to bring eight or nine horses to me. Of course, the local horses are brought, because it's easier just to walk one down the road or to hack it round the corner.'

The windows of the old smithy are thick with grime and cobwebs. The coals blaze and glow, and the shrill clang of the hammer on the anvil sends shock waves through your head. Behind the furnace some big, old-fashioned bellows blow air onto the fire as Graham operates them by hand. The sweat gleams on his face and arms. 'I have the original bellows in here, which I still use. They're the only ones of their kind left in the area – or even further afield, I should think. All the other local places have gone on to electricity, which personally I wouldn't have. I find the bellows are more controllable than what electric is. Yes, I think I'll use them until they wear out. The basics of shoeing horses hasn't changed virtually at all. The only thing is that the older shoes used to be a lot wider than what we use now. I believe as far back as the Romans and Egyptians horses were shod in the same way. And it's not changed much since.'

In a shed next door with a rough brick floor and white-washed walls, a handsome black gelding is fidgeting as it waits for its shoes. It shivers as it hears the fierce hiss of red-hot iron being plunged into water and looks wide-eyed over its shoulder as Graham arrives to fit the new shoe. 'It's virtually a seven day a week job. I just put myself on call, because I'm working with animals. Even Sundays I'll work, and

Christmas day if somebody wants me. Because the horses' comfort must come first. You can't leave animals in pain for long, if they've got problems with their feet. So you have to sort them out as soon as possible. You have to be a little bit of a psychologist. You have to try and assess what is wrong with the horse and why it's playing up. Sometimes it's nerves. Sometimes it's fear. Or sometimes it just doesn't want it done. You know, they're all different – like humans. They've got their moods, so they're going to have good days and they're going to have bad days. And, hopefully, we get them on the good days.'

As the black horse towers above him, Graham hammers home the last shoe and leans back to stretch his muscles. The horse tentatively tries the new shoe on the cobbled ground and then relaxes as it takes its weight without discomfort. Next door the bellows roar again as Graham prepares for his next customer.

YORKSHIRE accents and attitudes are not common on the South Downs. But John Gascoigne has headed south from his beloved country to play a part in preserving the beauty of the area. He is a big man with a sharp sense of humour. It is a tragedy that much of the south coast's splendour has been vandalised by third-rate planners and architects and by caravan camps. But, at the Seven Sisters Country Park, the tide of plastic progress has been turned back, thanks largely to the efforts of John Gascoigne who has been Head Ranger there for the last fourteen years. 'I came here in 1971. Everything was a challenge to start with. There were fights and rows. It's hard to believe now that everything seems so peaceful and settled.'

The voice has lost none of its North Country determination, and there is no trace of conversion to the smooth accents of the south. John points to the green flank of a hillside to the east of his patch. 'We made that. It used to be all tents when we came here. Seven hundred odd tents on that bit. Further down there were caravans. They'd been there for years. We had the pleasure of pulling 'em off and making it for the birds. It's clear of everything human now. So it's a good place . . . a fine place.'

He stared reflectively across to the sea, where the sun shines on the distant breakers. His piece of Sussex is where the river Cuckmere carves its way through the Downs into the English Channel. The high chalk towers on either side of the estuary where John Gascoigne and his team have created a naturalist's paradise. Here are rare flowers and plants; here waders feed on the mud as the tide goes down; and here are distant views, which have been unchanged for a thousand years and more. 'It's special and it's wonderful for the birds. The place is perfect for the waterfowl and waders. They are the birds that always used to be here. This part of the river was turned into a canal about a hundred and fifty years ago. So this is really artificial – artificially drained at least. So we had this inspiration of putting it back as it used to be. Well, that's true conservation, isn't it? Recreating the habitat that used to exist naturally. There's not a lot of water down here at the moment. We drain it off at the start of the winter to provide a bigger feeding area for the birds. And then, in the springtime, we flood it up to isolate the little islands for nesting.'

24

John Gascoigne's creation is a work of art. It is more beautiful than paintings or symphonies, and it is enjoyed by people of every class and background. Producing it has given him huge satisfaction, but, as a Yorkshireman, he is down to earth about it. 'Yes, it's beautiful all right. Better than a lot of caravans and a lot of tents anyway. It depends, of course. I mean, if you had a tent or a caravan, you probably think they are nice. But the tents and caravans had been here for a lot of years. So I think the birds can have the next fifty years. That's fair enough, isn't it?' And the big man smiles softly to himself as he climbs the steep side of the down to gaze out towards the Seven Sisters with the sea breaking relentlessly at his feet.

IN a deep fold of the downland near Rodmell, where Quentin Bell and the Bloomsbury group had their country retreat, lies Breaky Bottom Vineyard. This is reputed to be the warmest spot on the South Downs, and Di and Peter Hall live there on a farm that is reminiscent of those welcoming smallholdings in the French wine country. The warmth of the climate is one of the reasons for the excellence of their grapes and of the wine which they produce. The sun concentrates its heat in the hollow and, by October, the fruit is more yellow than green, and picking – with its non-stop routine as the precious juice is extracted and stored under Peter Hall's expert hand – is about to begin in earnest. 'At the moment we've got four acres. But it's not all producing yet. The vines come from the Loire and last year we managed to make 26,000 bottles of wine. What we try to do is to produce French wine in England. I'm half French and that, combined with the chalk on which the grapes grow and the warm temperatures, gives us a real chance to do this. By October, when the weather has been reasonably good through the year, we're poised to start harvesting. We're just waiting for the balance of the sugar and the acid to be perfect and then we're away. But waiting for that correct day is nerve-racking.'

During the long wait Di Hall also turns her talents to making and painting beautiful tiles. Down one side of the old farmyard and close to the barn where the wine is made and stored is a row of stables, which have been converted into her busy workshop. Here, designs are drawn, clay is pummelled and prepared, paints are mixed, and an old-fashioned press stands ready to do its duty.

'At the moment I'm making some mediaeval tiles for Lewes Priory to fit into a floor there. I was very lucky soon after I began to do this work, because a friend who is head of ceramics at an Art College said that he was going to give the beautiful tile-press they had to Brighton Engineerium. But then he thought how much better it would be to have it working, so that students could come and see tiles actually being made. He said that, provided I could move it, I could have it. But I had no idea how heavy it was going to be and how difficult it was going to be to transport it, even though it's quite small in size. Anyway, we managed, and now I spend what time I can find making mediaeval and Victorian acrostic tiles.'

And with her hands caked with clay and the heavy arm of the press swinging perilously through the air, Di continues to turn out her small works of art while the sun streams down tantalisingly on the steadily ripening grapes. 'It's the draw of the Downs that keeps me here – the fact that man has lived here for many, many centuries, and that we can go out walking on the hills, especially in the autumn when the fields are just ploughed. Each day is so different and so dramatic. It's a bit difficult sometimes, when you live here, to always appreciate just how beautiful it is.'

Breaky Bottom vineyard, in a fold of the downland near Rodmell, where Peter and Di Hall produce wine in what is reputed to be the warmest spot on the South Downs.

The red admiral is a most distinctive butterfly, with red bars on its wings and black wing tips spotted with white.

The Viper's Bugloss is a strikingly handsome plant found in chalkland areas, seen here against a background of the South Downs and the Seven Sisters cliffs.

The South Downs, which rise at Pevensey and run past Chichester, have some of the finest views in the country.

THE Harding family farm is not far from the South Downs and possesses many steep banks and wooded hillsides typical of the area. So the family is considering taking on a cart-horse to help with the heavy work around the farm. With this in mind, Marion Harding regularly makes the journey to Haremere Hall at Etchingham, where she can learn to handle, harness and work heavy horses. 'We haven't got a big horse yet, but I'm going to learn all about them, and then I hope we will. Mainly just 'cos I've always loved horses, I love working with animals generally and I think there are quite a few jobs that we could do with a horse on the farm.'

John Lavis, calm, wise and experienced, is in charge of the Shires, the Suffolk Punches, the Ardennes, the Clydesdales and the Welsh Cobs at Haremere Hall. On every side they are being used for farm work – ploughing, harrowing, transporting, hauling timber, and visitors can either come to watch and admire or to be taught.

'Our horses are part of our lives and are treated as such. They are quiet and well-behaved. We respect their dignity, their prowess and ability. We look after them and help them to the best of our ability if they are unwell. But we do not mollycoddle

29

or pamper them or treat them as pets. Ours is a partnership. We trust them and they trust us. They are members of their herd and their lives are geared to a known routine. They have their own form of society with their own patterns of behaviour, which we as human beings do well to respect. They are grazing animals, which do not cause harm to each other or to any other living creature. They do not torture, neither do they kill.'

Marion Harding confirms this view of the heavy horses as she does through her first difficult and tentative steps learning to work and to handle them. 'I've done some harnessing, driving and harrowing – things like that. But I haven't yet learned to train a horse. And I'm certainly going to need to learn a bit about that as well. Before this, I've worked with very high-spirited riding horses and really there's no comparison. I can't get over it. I keep expecting them to leap about and do stupid things, and they just don't seem to. They're very gentle.' As she talks the great, dark rumps stand in line in the stables. Every movement is slow and firm, and the smell is of hayfields and distant days of youth and tranquillity.

THE South Downs themselves seem as solid and as strong as the cart-horses of Haremere Hall. What creative and primaeval freak of fate can have flung such gently curving slopes with their fluted sides through the floor of the ocean, where once they lay? Such mountains appear nowhere else in the world, and today they stand on guard against the worst that wind and weather can throw at them. Rudyard Kipling loved these old hills, and captured their history in one short poem called *The Run of the Downs*.

'The Weald is good, the Downs are best –
I'll give you the run of 'em, East to West.
Beachy Head and Winddoor Hill,
They were once and they are still.
Firle, Mount Caburn and Mount Harry
Go back as far as sums 'll carry.
Ditchling Beacon and Chanctonbury Ring,
They have looked on many a thing,
And what those two have missed between 'em,
I reckon Truleigh Hill has seen 'em.
Highden, Bignor and Duncton Down
Knew old England before the Crown.
Linch Down, Treyford and Sunwood
Knew old England before the Flood;
And when you end on the Hampshire side
Butser's old as Time and Tide.
The Downs are sheep, the Weald is corn,
You be glad you are Sussex born!'

SELSEY

SELSEY sits at the tip of the Manhood Peninsula, the Southernmost part of Sussex, pointing like an arrowhead into the English Channel. Selsey, or Seal's Island, became joined to the mainland centuries ago. But today the sea is eating away at Selsey Bill, and at one time it was encroaching at the rate of six feet a year. If you have a vivid imagination, you can see the reason for the Manhood Peninsula's name in its physical shape. But some authorities say that Manhood is a corruption over the centuries of the words 'main wood', though it is difficult to picture any sort of forest or woodland if you visit the area today with its flat fields and open countryside.

The skill of fishing is supposed to have been brought to Sussex by St. Wilfrid, who landed at Selsey in 680 AD. He found the Saxon population dying from hunger and thirst after a long drought. Some were even being driven to drown themselves in the sea. The Saint taught them to fish with nets and, in this unspiritual way, converted them to Christianity. While he was baptising his first converts the weather broke at last and the rain fell. St. Wilfrid's Cathedral and monastery are now covered by the sea, and fishermen used to tell tales of hearing a bell beneath the waves when the wind was quiet. They also spoke of 'fishing in the Park' – a reference to a submerged deer park, which existed until the time of Henry VIII. Now there is just a small and remote Church for St. Wilfrid, about which Rudyard Kipling wrote a predictably charming Christmas poem:

> 'Eddi, priest of St. Wilfrid,
> In his chapel at Manhood End,
> Ordered a midnight service
> For such as cared to attend.
>
> But the Saxons were keeping Christmas
> And the night was stormy as well
> Nobody came to service
> Though Eddi rang the bell.
>
> "Wicked weather for walking"
> Said Eddi of Manhood End,
> "But I must go on with the service
> For such as care to attend".'

31

Alas, only a donkey and a bullock pushed their way into the isolated, little Church to escape from the foul weather.

'They steamed and dripped in the chancel,
They listened and never stirred,
While, just as though they were bishops,
Eddi preached them the word.

Till the gale blew off on the marshes
And the windows showed the day,
And the ox and the ass together
Wheeled and clattered away.

And when the Saxons mocked him,
Said Eddi of Manhood End –
"I dare not shut his chapel
On such as care to attend".'

Exposed as it is to the weather, Selsey can be a cold place to visit in the winter months. Snow, ice, frost, freezing fog and the brightest of bright sunshine are as common as the more normal grey, damp winter weather of southern England. In the cold the usually timid garden birds are uncannily tame – their fear of man overcome by their great hunger and their need for warmth. With their feathers puffed up like duvets to help them retain their body heat, they can be seen in the wild at closer quarters than at any other time. And the people of the area are as loyal to it, as proud and as self-contained as people in isolated communities always are.

WHEN he has a day off, fisherman Jamie Lawrence likes to go ferreting with his friend Mark Billingham and their two fine ferrets, Snowy and Percy. Jamie is tall and strong and lives in an old caravan in Selsey. His voice is soft and retains its quiet, Sussex accent. With his red beard, clear blue eyes and knitted hat he might be a pirate of old. But he is very gentle with the two strong, slim ferrets as he lifts them from their wooden cage. 'If you handle them regularly you can do virtually anything with them. They're just like a shooting-dog, if you treat them right. But, if you don't pick them up almost every day, they can get nasty and then they bite you every time you get near them. The two we've got we handle very often and we can do a lot with them. We've had quite a bit of trouble sometimes in the big hedges when we're out. Sometimes they go missing. So we've got a bleeper on one of the ferret's collars, so that we can just go along, pick up the signal and catch him. But the other one, if he decides to go walkabout, it takes a long time to find him. It's all guesswork. Every time the ferret pops his head out you've got to try and work out which way he's going to go next.'

The usual hunting-ground for Jamie and Mark is a field right on the edge of the village. Accompanied by an excited springer spaniel, the two men flush rabbits out of the surrounding brambles and frighten them towards a dense thicket in the middle of the field. Then they unwind a long, narrow net wound round strong sticks and surround the area with a rabbit-proof defence. Next the ferrets, struggling in their excitement, are lowered into gaps in the brambles. 'It's best to get up at crack of dawn really. The earlier you can get out the better, because, in that first hour or hour-and-a-half, you'll bolt more rabbits than you will the rest of the day. So every time we do go out early we always do well.'

Another of Jamie Lawrence's skills – handed down through his family – is to make traditional willow-pots for catching lobsters, crabs and particularly prawns. Sitting in front of his small fisherman's shed he weaves the bending sticks together into tough and attractive honeycomb pots. Around him are upturned boats and rows of newly-tarred and finished pots. Behind the bank of shingle, which rises twenty yards from where he is working, the waves break and carry the stones back and forward with their monotonous rhythm. The scene is as old as history and, only if you crane your neck can you see the new houses along the Selsey waterfront. 'There's not many of the old fellas left fishing now. There were three or four of them still on the go up to about two years ago. But there's only one old fella still goes out. We don't know how he does it, but he still does. I'm Selsey born and bred and generations before me, and I'd never leave the village – not ever. This is all I've ever done. Since I was four or five years old I used to go out in the boat with my father. And it's just like a disease really. The sea-water runs in your veins virtually. Where years ago it only used to be willow pots, it's mostly metal ones today. But most would agree that you want a willow pot to catch a prawn, and I'm about the only one who does it now. So this is why I'm going back to them, so that I can virtually have the prawning to myself.'

In a nearby hut a newly finished pot hangs dripping above a cauldron of tar, into which it has just been dipped. Out at sea the small boats toss and bob in the choppy waves and on the breakwaters small boys play and skip stones on the water. 'I fish up to about two miles off with the willow pots. I fish on ground that's been used by local families for generations – still in the same old spots. I suppose I could start using these metal pots – they do try and make them for catching prawns now. But they're not quite so good, even if they are a bit tougher than the willow.

'You see, a lobster won't cut up a willow pot too badly, but a crab will. If you don't get out there for a few days because the wind is blowing, and then the crabs get in, they're real devils and they'll virtually take a side out. And then you've got to bring the pot home and get it all mended up, which takes almost as long as it does to make a new pot.' And Jamie's strong hands fight the thin willow branches into shape as he sits on the step of his cluttered hut in the winter sunshine. His thoughts are far away at sea, and his calm face is impassive as he works.

SELSEY is world-famous for its lobsters and its fishermen are as tough and determined today as ever they were in the past. Nigel Osbourne and his partner Keith Lintock are out fishing all the year round – whenever the weather allows. In the winter months their sturdy motorboat chugs out to sea through the biting wind.

'The water temperature is cold now and what you've got to try and do is to drop your baited pot by a lobster, and hope he will just pop out of his hole. They won't walk any distance to a pot now where it's this chilly. But, of course, with lobsters, they'll not only walk in and out of their holes. They can also nip in and out of our pots. And this is specially true of lobsters, 'cos he swims where a crab crawls. And so a lobster's only got to keep flicking his tail and he'll eventually find the hole and make his way out.'

Nigel and Keith take it in turns to steer the boat from the relative warmth of the small top-heavy fo'c's'le. Whoever is not steering is cutting up and preparing bait. It is a freezing, ninety minute journey to the fishing grounds and, when they arrive, there is the heavy work of hauling in the pots, taking out the lobsters and measuring them to make sure that they are big enough to keep, rebaiting the pots and stacking them in neat piles on the deck of the little boat. They accomplish all of this with apparent ease in conditions which freeze the hands and numb the brain. Once, a floating rope thrown out by another lobster-boat fouls the propeller and Nigel plunges both arms into the sea for ten long minutes as he fights to clear the obstruction. At last the rope is cut free and fishing can continue.

'There's no special reason for the different shapes of the pots we use – some people prefer the creel and some people prefer the inkwell. But I don't think there's a great difference in what they catch. Really what you want is a pot with the smallest practical entrance hole, because obviously then there's a smaller space for the lobster to find and to escape through.'

On the wet and slippery surface of the deck the baited pots are fed back into the sea. The ropes lash and curl like enraged snakes as the weighted traps fall into the deep water. In the distance Selsey Bill sits comfortably on the horizon. 'You have to be very careful how you stack the pots, especially on a rough day. Because with blokes out on deck when the pots are going back over, if they grab the wrong one and you get a pile of rope and pots flying back to the stern, it could quite easily catch them and take 'em over the side. Quite often we have a bit of rope come along and twist your foot, and you have to be very quick. And the chap on the helm has to be handy with the knife just in case.'

As the boat turns and heads for home the seagulls wheel and scream behind it, diving into the sea for the scraps of left-over bait which have been thrown away. The sun, low in the sky all day, is sinking swiftly towards the horizon and golds and reds are beginning to streak the blue and to reflect gaudily in the water. It promises to be another frosty night and the two men hope for an untroubled journey to harbour. 'Some of the Selsey boys they fish way out to about nine miles, and they're fishing in 100 to 160 feet of water. Being the winter months we bring all the Selsey boats round into the harbour for protection from the weather. We ride them off the Bill during the summer, but the insurance companies won't risk the gamble off of Selsey during the winter and obviously we don't want to lose our vessels. So we work from Chichester, which makes a longer day for us. But you can sleep at night when the boat's safe.'

Back at Selsey Nigel and Keith settle down to their evening's work after their day's fishing. In an old warehouse, stacked to the ceiling with worn motorcar tyres, a group of men looking like latterday pirates, sit in a circle binding the bare, black frames of metal lobster-pots with thin strips of rubber. On one side of the building a venomous machine rips the tyres into tough rubber bandages. Opposite, working in an inadequate pool of light thrown by a naked bulb, the men grunt and curse as they wind the strips protectively round the shiny metal which has been turned into the skeletons of lobster-pots in a local factory.

'This year, whenever we've had the time, we've been earning a bit of extra cash working for a firm that produces lobster-pots. We put them together and rubber them and get them ready for the fishermen to dump straight into the sea. It saves them the aggravation of having to make them themselves, and gets us a bit of beer money.' And, as darkness falls outside and the bright moon lights up the streets, the strong arms tug at the rubber and the mouths grimace with the effort of the work.

JUST to the north of Selsey stands Coles Farm House, a magnificent old country mansion, a bit run down now, but still carrying its faded grandeur with pride. It is the home of wheelwright, coach-maker and craftsman, George Upfold – a burly old man with a quick sense of humour and rugged artist's hands. He uses ancient tools with a skill that may well vanish within a generation. His work speaks for itself. It is meticulous in its detail and fine in its finish.

'I was a bound apprentice. I did five years as an apprentice and two as an improver. And then, in those days, I was earning eight shillings a week and over those seven years I was travelling twenty miles either way each day. I was only late once due to fog. I was late by five minutes and I was stopped half-an-hour of my wages! The coach I'm building at the moment is more of a challenge than anything else. Once I've finished this one, I don't think I'll be doing any more in that line. But I'll make other things to bring the pennies in and to keep going. A coach is really a big challenge and a whole lot of work. I know, 'cos I've built 'em in the past.'

The coach stands in the silent workshop. The wheels and the frame are complete, and the body is beginning to grow. It is a strange sight to see such an old-fashioned carriage being newly built in the 1980s. On the work benches beneath the planes and saws, which hang on the walls, stand exquisite, miniature chests and chairs and tables. 'These models I make I prefer to call travellers' samples. Because all these pieces – chairs, chests-of-drawers and all – were carried round by the travellers to the estates to show the potential customer what could be made. Of course, this was

George Upfold, wheelwright and coachmaker, making a 'sociable' carriage. He uses ancient tools with a skill that may vanish within a generation.

before they had those glossy magazines. And now these miniatures themselves sell. In fact, they're much sought after.'

In the elegant rooms of the old farm house stand magnificent grandfather clocks, as many as three or four in a room. Everything about them confirms that they must be genuine antiques, but they are, in fact, the work of George Upfold's talented hands. The inlaid woodwork and the perfect finish come from another age. 'The clocks that I specialise in are copied from old long-cased ones. I had the original movements and I built the cases round them according to the old design. It's very satisfying work.' And the old face softens as the eyes critically examine the workmanship.

BLUEY is a small but strong twelve year old Exmoor pony, now living in Park Lane, Selsey. He is a loyal member of the Pearson family and goes swimming with them in the sea in the summer-time. He lives in a hut at the bottom of the garden and likes an occasional pint of beer, turkish delight and roses, but not necessarily all at the same time. For Mrs Pearson he is also a willing porter as he accompanies her to the bank and then to the greengrocer to buy vegetables. Part of the agreement with Bluey is that an extra pound of carrots is included for him.

'He's very useful and helpful. For instance, a friend of mine does my hair for me. So we barter, and I take her children for a ride. All kinds of things like that. I want some glass for a window that's broken. Okay, somebody's got it, so I take them out in the pony and trap. He's a very valuable fellow. In the summer he is really blue. He goes a roan blue. In the spring he's grey, and he's lovely and smooth-coated in the summer. So he makes life interesting all the year round. What he hates is the cold wind and rain. They make him very unhappy. But he always puts fun into life because, as you go around, people smile at you.'

As snow begins to fall Bluey trots off to town pulling the family in the trap behind him. The landscape is white and silent and the short hoof-beats echo across the fields. He is on his way to visit Dave Lawrence, the Selsey blacksmith and farrier. In addition to shoeing Bluey and the local horses, Dave repairs and makes equipment for the fishermen. His smithy is full of the usual clutter of a forge, except that here there are wicked-looking sea anchors with deep, sharp teeth and every sort of metal instrument, which modern fishing demands. 'Selsey originated from four or five families – the Arnolds, the Woodlands, the Lawrences and the Sherringtons. My great great grandfather was the first coxswain of the Selsey lifeboat. It was all rowing in those days and harder than anything we dream of.'

Bluey waits patiently outside in the snow while Dave heats up the shoes and hammers them into shape. At a table nearby iron name-plates are being cut out and everywhere there is smoke and steam and bustle. 'I don't think you could make a living today at shoeing here like you would years ago. There are still quite a lot of horses about, but then there are a few more blacksmiths travelling around. So we do wrought-iron work and we mend all the fishermen's equipment, and make all the grappling irons and things like that for them.' The snow falls steadily, blotting out sight and sound and, as Bluey trots homewards, you could easily imagine that you were deep in the Russian steppes and that the wolves were closing in. Bluey's thoughts, however, are on his stable and his hay.

NORTH-EAST of Selsey lies Pagham harbour. Today it is a harbour in name only, and just yachtsmen sail its smooth waters. But in the Middle Ages Pagham was prosperous and the population far bigger than it is now. By the 19th century the harbour had become blocked and farming took over much of the land. But in 1910 a mighty storm broke down the sea wall and turned the harbour into what it is today – a yacht basin and wildlife sanctuary, which is a goal for wild-fowlers and bird-watchers from all over the world. It is ideally placed for birds migrating to the north or to the south and particularly for the dark-bellied brent goose, of which 10% of the world population comes here in the winter. Tall and bearded, Bob Lord is the wildlife warden, who is in charge of the area.

'There's always something to see here at any time of the year. Particularly in the winter, of course, when it's very hard, very cold conditions and there's lots of snow around and lots of ice. The tide's just going down, so the birds that have been at roost are coming to the edge to feed on the soft mud which is exposed. Once the mud has been covered over by the sea-water the small invertebrates tend to come to the surface of the mud and, as the tide goes back down again, birds come to the edge to feed. They're picking up all the juicy, soft worms that are living down in the mud. Also, in these conditions when it is very, very cold they tend to come down to the edge for another reason as well. They can find shelter in all the vegetation along the shore.'

One of the sad but true facts of bird-watching is that the best times to see birds at close quarters are usually the most uncomfortable times for human beings. Bob Lord seems unaware of the bitter conditions as he strides across the snow and ice to see what is stirring. 'There's plenty of small wading birds feeding down here. They come from areas much further north than anywhere in Great Britain. Many of them breed in the Arctic Circle within the tundra regions where it's probably the temperature it is here now at the end of August or the beginning of September. If the conditions elsewhere in this country are exceptionally cold, birds tend to fly down to the south coast, where there's plenty of feeding for them on the salt marshes and it's relatively mild. Birds in this weather always look very fat. It's not that they've been feeding well, though they're obviously going to eat everything they can find. It's the fact that they've fluffed up their feathers to keep a layer of air between their skin and their outer feathers, to keep them as warm as possible. It's like a sort of portable string vest.' As he walks off across the frozen beach the birds move slowly aside, apparently unafraid or too intent on their search for food to fly off into the chilly dusk.

IN spite of modern buildings and intensive farming there is still much that is unspoilt on the flatlands of the Manhood Peninsula. But perhaps here, as anywhere else in Sussex, the last word should belong to Rudyard Kipling, whose love of the county resulted in some of his most enthusiastic poems:

> 'God gives to men all earth to love
> But, since man's heart is small,
> Ordains for each one spot shall prove
> Beloved over all.
> Each to his choice, and I rejoice
> The lot has fallen to me —
> In a fair ground, in a fair ground,
> Yea, Sussex by the sea.'

RYE

RYE, in East Sussex, is in every way a picture postcard town. Perched on a sandstone rock, it is surrounded by the sea on one side and by the rivers Brede, Rother and Tillingham on the other three. The name originates from an old term which was used to describe a bleak island, and Rye itself was once just such an island, joined to the mainland by a narrow strip of beach. Thus, over the centuries, the marshland emerged from the sea only to be swallowed up again when terrible storms flooded the area. A verse from *The Lost Harbours of Sussex* describes it:

'There rolls the deep where grows the tree,
O earth, what changes hast thou seen.
There where the long street roars hath been
The stillness of the central sea.'

Before the Romans arrived there was a strategic ridgeway leading from the estuary and passing inland near Rye and Old Winchelsea, through Cripps Corner, Netherfield and Heathfield to Uckfield, before joining the Lewes to London Way. This track was used for transporting iron from the works at Battle and Sedlescombe down to the estuary for shipment.

During the Hundred Years War there were terrible attacks by the French on Rye. In 1377 the town was left a smoking ruin. And in 1378 a petition addressed to Richard II asked him 'to have consideration of the poor town of Rye, inasmuch as it had been several times taken . . . and is unable further to repair the walls, wherefor the town is, on the sea side, open to enemies'. That same year a joint raid of retaliation was made on the French by the men of Rye and Winchelsea, during which the church bells of Rye, which had been taken during the major French attack, were retrieved. In *The Worthies of England* Fuller describes it thus. 'The English raiders took all such prisoners who were able to pay ransom and, amongst the rest, they took out of the steeple the bells and brought them back to England – bells which the French had taken formerly from these towns and which afterwards did ring the more merrily, restored to their proper place with addition of much wealth for the cost of their recovery.'

John Wesley came to Rye in 1773 and wrote in his diary 'I set out for Sussex and found abundance of people willing to hear the good word, at Rye in particular. And

The charming town of Rye was once an island connected to the mainland by a strip of beach, and was a centre of the smuggling trade.

they do many things gladly, but they will not part with the accursed thing, smuggling.' It is hardly surprising that one of Kipling's most famous poems is based on the darker side of this charming place:

> 'Five and twenty ponies trotting through the dark,
> Brandy for the parson, baccy for the clerk,
> Them that asks no questions isn't told a lie,
> Watch the wall my darling while the gentlemen go by.'

THE fishermen of Rye are a race apart. It is a dangerous coast and, when the weather is tolerable, the fishing fleet is out and at work at hours that would cause a strike in any other industry. The men are hard and strong and loyal to each other. Michael Paine, who by himself pilots and fishes from a forty foot boat, is no exception. 'I got up at two today. The wife levered me out of bed. I come down on the boat, came to sea, got out the end of the harbour and someone had lowered the curtains. The fog was as thick as a hedge. It was like that till nine o'clock I suppose. Just running on radar.'

From the harbour a narrow channel, just wide enough for two fishing boats to pass in opposite directions, runs straight out to sea. On the way home the old town sits comfortingly on its tall rock in front of you and the fish-market bustles with activity. On the way out there is nothing but the wind and the waves and the back-breaking work ahead. 'In the summer we are in fairly shallow water, almost up to the beach at times, for Dover soles. But in winter we are in anything from ten to twenty-five fathoms. Some people go off fishing and they're happy with whatever comes up in the net. One fellow I know likes to catch whiting. Now they can drop down to about a pound or eighty pence a stone when they're in full swing. Whereas I'd prefer to go and get the same number of individual soles and still make the same money. Although I'd only land maybe a box of fish and he's landing twenty boxes, at the end of the day and the bottom of the ticket, it would be the same money.'

Out in the deep, cold water Michael Paine leaves the helm and moves down to the winding gear which coughs into action, and slowly lowers the nets from their position hanging high in the stern, into the sea. The whole operation takes him about five minutes and, at the end, the metal hausers tremble as they take the strain. The boat's engine changes its note under the weight that it is pulling, and gulls hover curiously overhead. They seem to float in the slipstream with barely a wing-beat and they move their heads inquisitively from side to side. 'The job's getting more and more difficult. For ten years there hasn't been a vast increase in the price of fish, including sole and plaice, but everything else – diesel, gear and insurance – shoots up every year. Least, that's what it looks like from here.'

After half an hour of trawling the nets are laboriously winched in. Excitement mounts among the gulls as the heavy load comes aboard. With a flick of a lever Michael dumps the writhing mass of fish, seaweed and some bits of debris onto the deck, which is turned into an ice rink for the unwary. And the fisherman sits on an upturned box and begins to sort through his catch with methodical care. As he throws the rejected fish over the side the pursuing gulls dive and squabble and scream with delight.

'It's not just the fishermen who can look vicious. Some of the things we catch can be pretty nasty too. There's an angler fish. If he's in amongst the catch and you're kicking it about with your boots and you put your foot in his mouth, it makes you hop all right. That is if he's light enough to lift. Otherwise you're trapped, like a man-trap. But the main danger for us is when we're heading back home and there's a blow. Trouble is then that you get a lot of ground swell. You've got to wait more than your normal time to be able to get in without hitting the bar at the end of the channel. It feels like concrete if you hit it, although it's only sand.'

As Michael Paine's boat chugs down to the fish-market to unload, skeletons of old ships stand on the skyline. Little creosoted huts lean on the muddy banks, and it is possible to imagine this same place over two hundred years ago when Lord

Pembroke asked: 'Will Washington take America, or the smugglers England first? The bet would be a fair even one.' For in those days England was a nation of smugglers.

WITH this tradition of smuggling and fishing behind it, it is no surprise that Rye is known in many countries for the quality of its boat-building. The ancient crafts have been handed down through the generations, and Harry Phillips and his family still run a thriving boatyard on the edge of the marshland. 'I was born here – right on the spot nearly where the yard is. And the town itself has changed a tremendous lot in that time. On the river in front of our boatyard the trawlers used to come along and tie up and the barges carrying cheese, gravel, coal, timber and all manner of things. Now, of course, it all comes by road and only the fishing boats operate.'

Although he has passed on the work of the yard to his son, Harry still takes an inquisitive interest in everything that is happening. Inside the workshop brass and copper rivets are being hammered, wood shaped and trimmed, and two sturdy, wide boats are slowly taking shape under the expert hands of the local craftsmen. Everything is precise and nothing is left to chance. 'We call it a beach-boat, specially designed for the beach, 'cos they've got a very fine, very blunt forefoot – that bit as you come round the stem. In the old days that was very blunt, so when they came ashore with the surf behind them they'd shoot up the beach. 'Cos, of course, they only had a lugsail, never had engines in 'em in them days, you know. You had to row the darn thing.'

Just as the building of boats has changed with the arrival of power saws and electricity, so the boats themselves have changed with the coming of engines. But the work involved is still just as skilled and the craftsmanship even greater. 'Since engines the forefoot has to be much finer or else they would pound so much and smash 'em all up the forefoot, you see. And the timbers and keels used to be all oak – locally grown not far away. Wych-elm for the boats. Wych-elm's like gold. It really is. And now it's been butchered and cut down and never been replaced. That's the trouble. It takes a long time to grow, wych-elm does. Some of it's been coming here from right the way down Devon, Cornwall and that way.

Lot of people thinks you wants wych-elm especially. But it must be fifty-fifty. Or else when you rivet it together and it gets wet – if it was too dry before – then it stretches the copper nails and, when it settles down, 'course you got a boat that's like a sieve all the time. A lot of people have made that mistake. When they've asked us about it we've told 'em it has to be fifty-fifty and they don't believe us. Not 'till they've built it and find out afterwards. People don't realise it, but we don't have no drawings for these boats. Nothing. People just tell us what they want and we build it for them. It's been in the family for years and years, that design.'

In the last century almost the whole of Rye was engaged in shipbuilding in one way or another, with yards stretching from the Strand to the eastern end of the Rock

Derek Phillips at the family boatyard at Rye where they continue to make boats using time-honoured methods and traditional materials.

Channel. A report at the time said that '. . . many remarkably fine vessels have been launched from our Rye slips, which have been greatly admired for their beautiful model, but more particularly for their excellent sailing qualities'. Harry Phillips and his team continue the tradition and keep up the high standards of their ancestors.

EVERY winter Wednesday the marsh farmers come to Rye to sell their sheep at the market at the bottom of the town. The meat gets its special flavour from the salt on the sea-grasses and, although it is only a small and old-fashioned sale, it is still full of energy and excitement. The sheep huddle together in the pens. Men push their way through to clip their ears, and the crowd of butchers and other buyers follow the auctioneer down the alley-ways as he calls the prices and the odds.

Local farmer Bill Cook is a regular at the sales. 'This market has been going since 1859. I can remember small farmers would bring in butter and eggs and everything was very different in those early days. It's all sheep now. There was a time when there was cattle, sheep and pigs. But it's just sheep alone now. They come from all over Romney Marsh and quite a lot too up into the Weald areas like Northiam and as far away as Battle probably. We've got Kents, South Downs, Dorsets, Suffolk

43

crosses, Dutch crosses, North country greyfaces. There's a tremendous variety. When I first started here there would have only been South Downs and Kents. So it's a very big change. But there's still more Romney ewes – or Kents as we call them – than any other breeds round here still.' And Bill turns and watches as scores of sheep scramble up the ramp of an old truck on their way to the slaughterhouse. By lunchtime the market is empty and quiet again and the local pubs are doing brisk and noisy business.

THE local Rye clay has been used by potters over the centuries. It tempted Wally Cole down from London after he was demobbed at the end of the war. And today he is part of a thriving industry. At The Rye Pottery, where he works, ranks of Canterbury Pilgrims, robins, mugs and plates stand in jumbled profusion. Wally bends over his whirling wheel and, as if by magic, a shapely bowl grows under his hands. 'We were once digging our clay on the marsh just close to the sea. And then, about twenty odd years ago now, the sea tried to come back over the marsh and they built this enormous sea wall. After that we were all stopped digging this side of it in case we weakened the wall. So then we had to go further afield, and we brought in a white clay from Cornwall and a red clay from Devon, and we mixed them so that they were the same colour as our local clay.'

Wally's foot moves up and down, with a steady rhythm as the bowl grows and becomes smooth. His head bends close to his work and the old, stained hands move and shape the clay with the sure touch of years of experience. 'We're foreigners really and truly. We only came here in 1947 after the war. You have to be born in Rye to be a Ryer. But it was good to be out of London. I threw my first pot in 1930, and I've always worked on a kick-wheel. I personally think that there is a closer harmony between your mind and your foot on a kick-wheel than on the machine one. But that's just personal preference.'

In another small room three artists are painting Canterbury Pilgrims. The concentration is intense. The only sound is the brush moving across the porous surface of the clay. It is no joke colouring a score of identical pottery figures in a day. 'It's like painting on blotting paper. As soon as you touch a wet brush to the dry powder it sucks it in. So you can't alter it. You can't make mistakes. The decorators have to get very dextrous in doing just what is wanted and then leaving it.'

The hard, detailed work continues. The Christmas trade for the famous pottery is brisk. But it is in the summer tourist season that business booms, and the winter months are spent preparing for that onslaught.

AT the top of the town Alan Webb is up before first light, along with the Rye fishermen. But his task is to bake bread and to make cakes. His old bakery is a magnet for the townspeople and, of course, for the summer tourists. Just to walk in the door is enough to make you hungry as the unforgettable smell of freshly baked bread fills the air and penetrates to the most diet-conscious stomach. 'Obviously I

Selsey beach, at the southernmost tip of Sussex. Selsey is world-famous for its lobsters.

The late Jack Lewis, gamekeeper and village elder. His vast knowledge and experience of country matters helped keep alive the time-honoured traditions of his village.

think that it's a skilled job. I get up at half-past four every morning, apart from the weekends. I get up at half-past two on Saturday mornings – a bit earlier. But then Saturday is a different sort of day. We tend to make only the bread and morning stuff on a Saturday. Confectionery lines are usually done beforehand and baked off on a Saturday morning. But the hard work's done in advance, and we don't stay longer than about ten or eleven o'clock Saturday morning. We do it all by hand, apart from the mixing. All the moulding and scaling is done by hand here.'

Alan is hard at work decorating a perfect, round Christmas cake, and his hands are steady as he applies the frills and colours to the smooth, white surface. Behind him, one of his colleagues pulls rows of loaves, shaped like hedgehogs, out of the black depths of the big oven with its old wrought-iron front. In the shop the people of Rye queue and chatter as they buy their bread and succumb to the temptation of cakes and buns.

'We suspect that the oven is the original one. The firm whose name appears over the top is Smith and Son. They are an old-established firm of oven-builders and they've recently gone out of business. But they did the present conversion to gas firing. And Mr Smith considered that the brickwork of the oven was older than the front and that the front had at some time been renewed. So the brickwork is likely original – probably around two hundred years old, which ties up with the little sign on the front of the shop that says it's 260 years old. I've also seen documentary evidence of this building being a bakery in 1779.'

With great care Alan picks up the finished cake and puts it in a place of honour in the window. Small boys passing by stop and stare with hungry eyes.

IT is likely that strange faces have been treated with suspicion and mistrust in Rye ever since 450 AD when the area was shut in by the Saxons and the Jutes on the east and west, by the sea in the south and by impenetrable forest in the north. In this part of Sussex today people are still reticent, especially with strangers. With good reason, for one Rye citizen said that if hell was like his town in the summer when the visitors were there, then he would change his ways immediately. In the winter months it is, nevertheless, a beautiful, peaceful and eccentric place – the sort of town where a local lad can take his pet llama for its daily walk through the busy crowds of shoppers without causing any apparent surprise.

BALCOMBE

THERE is still a sense of 'times forgotten' in the little village of Balcombe on the borders of East and West Sussex. It lies not far from the open expanse of Ashdown Forest, where Winnie the Pooh made his home. Although Gatwick Airport is close to the north; although the main Brighton to London railway runs past the village; and although many of the fine, old houses have been bought by wealthy London commuters, there is still plenty of rural calm and countryside character. There is also a community spirit and a feeling of history which is disappearing from so many small places within travelling range of big cities.

TUCKED away on Bowders Farm – just outside the village – is the cottage where retired game-keeper and village elder, Jack Lewis, used to live. Jack died in his eightieth year on the night of December 8th, 1985. He was buried on a wet and blustery day in the old churchyard a few days later, and most of the villages turned out to say good-bye. Jack's knowledge and experience of country ways and country moods was broad and full of wisdom and he and his family formed a core of those who helped to maintain village life in the old style.

Jack was a tall, upright old man with the ginger in his hair only just beginning to fade. That red hair gave warning that there might be quite a temper beneath the warm-hearted and hospitable exterior. And certainly there was strength and power in everything he did. The north country accent remained, though it had mellowed through years of contact with soft southerners. The eyes were shrewd and summed up strangers swiftly. Jack was seldom rude to fools or sycophants, but he saw through them swiftly and intuitively. Straight of back and strong of limb right up to the end, he died in his bed on a cold winter's night with his three beloved golden retrievers around him.

Jack's early life moulded him. He grew up in Congleton in Cheshire at the beginning of the century. The town had a reputation for being a place where women worked and men did not. His mother laboured in the mills and his father was a soldier, who became Regimental Sergeant-Major in the Cheshire Regiment in the First World War. 'I spent all my early days in a very rough community. The children were tough. The people were poor.'

Jack Lewis learnt many valuable lessons from his childhood, and his philosophy will strike a chord with those who believe that this country has deteriorated through softness and comfort. 'If you've got some guts and determination, you can do almost anything. A young chap should never belittle himself. He's just as good as the next chap. He's better if he thinks he's better and he shows he's better. I'd never had no real education. Nor did my father. But he was a better educated man than me. I remember that he was the most marvellous writer. He educated himself. So did me mother. Today they get education thrown at 'em, and I know lots and lots of young chaps as have been to various good schools and colleges and their writing is almost unreadable. And they can't converse. They can't tell you what their troubles are. Education's cost a lot of money, but it hasn't done a lot of good. Everything's too easy now. We don't have to work for anything. I remember poor boys at my school. I mean really poor. Boys that never wore shoes and stockings. They went to school with nothing on their feet, because they hadn't got anything. And their clothes were only cut-down pieces of cloth what somebody had thrown away. Now some of those boys were really good, and went on to good jobs – jobs of standing. They did well in military careers – in the army and the navy. Anything where there was competition, they did well. And I think a lot of it was to do with that, when I was a little boy, if you had anything, somebody took it off you. But if you wanted to live you took good care they didn't take it off you. You stuck up for yourself.'

In the last years of his life Jack spent much of his time looking back, often with pleasure and sometimes in distinguished company. 'I think everybody's thoughts go back and I've no doubt about it that, in everybody's life, some part of their young lives was the best. I talked to a very prominent man – as a matter of fact he became Prime Minister – and I had a day with him out shooting, and he talked to me at length of his boyhood days. He really enjoyed them. And so did I. And I think it's good to look back, whatever it's been, whether it's been rough or smooth. If it's been rough you think, "Well, I did well to weather that".'

Another lasting impression from Jack's childhood was the effect that drink had on the miners and farmworkers who lived in his neighbourhood. It was the usual thing for them to get drunk on Saturday night, when they would fight and 'belt' the women. 'Well, I'm an old man now, but in those young days I saw so much trouble and so much strife that I made a vow to meself that I would never drink. And I've never tasted beer in me life, and that's a fact. Nor spirits. All because of that time when I saw these men and they got drunk and they hit their women. They hit the children. They shouted and they swore. It wasn't my kettle of fish. I didn't like it. So I thought to meself, "Well, I won't join that lot". And I didn't.'

Snow came to Balcombe during the January of Jack's last year. Every day and several times each day the old man marched out through the blizzards and the ice to feed the flocks of ducks, geese, pheasants, chickens, guinea-fowl, peacocks and peahens, as well as the swarms of small garden birds, which treated his home in their hundreds as an hospitable sanctuary. Dressed in warm clothes, he looked like a throw-back to the Middle Ages – a stalwart peasant farmer. And the birds, in their hunger, showed no fear or distrust of him or of his impeccably trained dogs. 'When it snows there's a bewildered expression on them. They don't know what it is. And it takes days and days for them to get used to it. It affects them in several ways, but I think the main thing is that they take it for granted that they're far better sitting where they are than worrying and looking for stuff. I think they accept it better than we do. I feed so many for so long. I don't think I can do any more. The majority of birds around here will come to where I am. I've not got to go and look for them. If they know there's a food supply, distance doesn't matter. If you clear a place in an acre of ground and put some food down they will come to it, they find a way to converse and they tell the others.' As he speaks a new flight of ducks sails in through the snow-flakes. They waddle self-importantly forward and begin to help themselves.

It is not just the birds that suffer in cold weather. All living creatures have urgent and often unexpected problems. 'I was farm manager at one time, and I had some cattle, ten heifers and a bull, in a field. And it was terrible weather. I went out one morning and there were icicles on them. It had snowed and thawed and then it had frozen up again and the icicles were under the belly – some of them a foot long. And I didn't know what to do. So I made a shed out of tin and put some straw in it. But those cows never went in it. The only time they used it was in the summer time to get out of the way of the flies. And they laid out on the open field and it was terrible, terrible weather. And every morning they had icicles on them.'

It is probably no exaggeration to say that Jack's three best friends were his dogs, although human visitors came to his cottage all the time and always found a cup of tea or a meal and a welcome. Jack walked the dogs as though they were athletes in training and fed them like champions. For a special treat he made them lie on their backs and then scratched their tummies with a spiky besom. In return he expected good manners and instant obedience, and he also received a non-stop abundance of affection.One of his favourite walks was along the side of a meadow with huge, glistening Balcombe reservoir as a backdrop. Ancient oaks grow in the rich pasture, and the old man strode out, walking stick in hand, with his tweed hat low on his forehead. Around his feet the dogs moved and jostled, each in search of the favoured position at his heel.

'Well, they're all part and parcel of my set-up. Anna's nearly ten and I've got her two pups here. Angus, which is a super dog and his sister, which is called several names and a damned nuisance sometimes. Their main thing in life is going out shooting and sleeping. And, in between, a good feed. We all four live together in the cottage. I do all the chores and they do damn all. I mean, they make a helluva mess and don't clean up at all. I even find the food for them. They eat it. But I get a tremendous amount of pleasure out of 'em. They make horrible noises and worse smells when they've had a good feed. But I don't suppose they can help it. They don't seem to worry about it. We get on very well together. They're great company. And they've never answered me back yet.

'They're a very good type of golden retriever. They're placid and they're well-

The late Jack Lewis at Bowders Farm with two of his retrievers. One of his hobbies was to whittle wood into walking sticks with handles carved in the shape of animal heads which he accomplished with great skill.

behaved. Angus is a big, strong dog and he retrieves a cock pheasant and he loves it. He never hurts 'em. He'll bring five or six pheasants, which have been shot and probably had a wing broken and run off, and they've got to be retrieved. This is part of his job. He's got to find that pheasant, otherwise it would die and have a horrible end. And he will find the pheasant, pick it up and bring it to me, so that it can be killed. And he never hurts 'em, never knocks a feather off. He's so tender. The same dog will pick up a little chicken at a day old, and he won't hurt it. And he'll even bring me an egg, his mouth's so soft. And this is the great thing about all three of them. They don't hurt anything.'

As gamekeeper on the local estate Jack's dogs were an essential part of his work. After his retirement his son John succeeded him in the job. But Jack still loved to go out with Angus during the shoots to help retrieve wounded birds, to beat and to enjoy the company. It is ideal pheasant-shooting country in this part of Sussex with steep banks, thick cover, wide open spaces and broad rides through woodland. The guns travel in a farm trailer, sitting on bails and with a canvas cover to protect them

51

from the weather. The beaters move slowly through the woods, their cries echoing among the trees. And the dogs are on the move on all sides – tense, excited and longing for action. 'It's their nature to hunt and to catch things, isn't it? I mean, why does a fox love hunting a rabbit? He really loves it. And when he's caught it he'll throw it up in the air and he'll gloat over it. I've seen them. When they catch a pheasant they love it too and play with it, unless they're very hungry. The first thing they do then is to eat it. Sometimes it's the same thing with a dog. They were once wild and they've been tamed by human beings and we've trained them. We could train a fox the same if we went to the same trouble. And you can teach a dog without being cruel at all. All this hitting dogs and shouting at them is useless. But they will do almost anything for kindness. And if you understand them and go into their lives, you'll find that they're much more clever than they're given credit for. They're certainly cleverer than some humans I know.'

Jack gently fondled the ears of the little one, the least obedient of the three. And she looked up at him as though she wished she could die for him at that moment. 'I'll give you an instance, and this happened just recently. I was digging in me garden, quite a way from the house, and I'm growing a bit deaf and I heard the dog howling. So I put me spade down and came to the back door, and the telephone was ringing. I answered it and the man said that he'd been ringing for ages. So I said that I was sorry, but that I had been in the garden and that I hadn't heard it. Two or three days after, the same thing happened. I was chopping wood and I heard me dogs howling. So I came in and the telephone was ringing again. And now this little dog, if I'm not indoors and if the telephone rings, she will come to the door and howl. She doesn't bark, just howls. I think it's wonderful. Now I'm sure I could train that dog to tell me practically anything. Obviously, how it's come about, I've been sitting indoors, the telephone's rung and I've jumped up. I try to answer it quickly, because you never know if it's an emergency, and they've all jumped up as well. We've all gone to the telephone together. So when I've not been there, the little dog has thought, "Well, I'd better do something about this". And she has.'

One of Jack's great skills was to carve and whittle sticks and to turn them into works of art. The small rooms of his cottage were full of stout walking-sticks with coloured handles – ducks and pheasants heads, badgers and foxes, cows and horses and owls. On winter evenings he would sit by his fire, his spectacles on his nose and a dead pheasant's head as a model on the arm of his chair, chipping away at the wood with a chisel, an old razor blade and pieces of broken glass. He could probably have sold the sticks for good money. But he never did. He either gave them away or he kept them.

'You want to cut your wood about Christmas time. It wants to be cut, put in a shed and forgot about for at least a year. It's no good cutting it when it's green because the sap crinkles it and it's soft. You must cut it in the winter time when the sap's down. That goes for hazel, ash and a bit of cherry if you like. But the holly, which makes some of the best sticks, that wants to be cut at the end of

April or May, when its sap is down. And that goes for laurel and all the evergreens too.'

Jack walked off down to the winter woods with the dogs scampering around him. The frost was on the growing corn and the sun was a deep red and low on the horizon. The old man walked looking sharply from side to side. When he saw something that seemed hopeful, he would plunge into the thicket. The dogs raced in after him expecting to find a rabbit or a pheasant. They looked disappointed when they discovered that he was only after sticks again.

'You need a stick with a straight shank and a decent piece of wood growing out of the root or with a thick branch. The bit growing out wants to be as thick as your leg with a good, strong stick growing up from it about five feet long. When you cut it off you cut the thick piece six inches each side of the stick – like a T with a fat cross-piece. If you cut it say two inches each side of the stick it will crack in the process of drying and be no good for carving. The important thing is what is in your imagination when you pull it up. It's if you can see something in the stick. And it may be that you've seen a horse's head or a dog's head or a Harry Lauder stick in it. And you try it and it's probably quite good.' The old cracked hands worked slowly and gently and with infinite care and patience. The logs crackled in the grate. Slowly the unmistakable shape of a pheasant's head began to emerge from the wood. He was making a pair of sticks – a cock and a hen pheasant – as a special wedding present for his old boss's son and his bride.

The spring of 1985 was late and cold in Sussex after the hard and frosty winter. Jack Lewis's main concern was for his garden, which was his pride. To say that he grew everything would be an exaggeration, but a list of what he did not grow would be short and dull. In season his half-acre was ablaze with flowers and fruit and vegetables – all grown professionally and to perfection. A mighty vine twined its way around the house. Giant green and purple gooseberries grew beside mighty marrows. And upstairs in Jack's bedroom, prize potatoes were stored away for the winter months. 'I suppose you enjoy springtime most when you're old. You haven't got that zest what the young man's got to look for something extra. You just feel you've got through a winter and you know you've got the summer coming. I've got several things which have to be done in the garden. I've got muck to put on, which is quite a lot of heavy wheeling about with the wheelbarrow. I've got a fence, which protects some of the flowers, to mend. It's made of hazel and its lifetime is about two, sometimes three years. Then it wants renewing. And of course the dogs try to get through it and one of the uprights breaks off and then your fence is done. So I've got to start afresh and re-do the whole thing, which wants getting on with before I get too busy in the garden itself. So that's one of the main jobs. Another job is to get me bean-sticks. I can't go and cut those when the sap's coming up. They should all be cut before March 25th, tied up and brought ready. I've also got pea-sticks to cut, which also have to be done before the leaf shows or the sap runs up. All these are jobs that I've got to do before getting on with the garden itself. You see, you can't dig when it's wet, and you can't plant your seeds when it's wet. So these other things, such as mending me fence and doing me sticks and that, all can come in when it's not fit to do the garden itself.

'A lot of the digging is delayed this year because of the frost. But now I've managed to get on quite a lot with it and, given a few days dry sunshine, it's all more or less ready for planting. I was very surprised earlier. I started to do some digging and found the frost was in four inches, a good four inches deep. So that had to be left, cos you don't never dig with frost in your garden. Anyway, I let the frost go and did some digging and I was able to put three rows of early potatoes in on February 27th, which I thought was quite good. I also put in some bulbs on the 20th of February and I see they're just about beginning to peep through the ground.'

Jack spent hundreds of hours each month in his garden and never appeared to get bored or tired by the steady, back-breaking toil. He always spoke of it with satisfaction. 'The rest of me garden is in the process now of being ready for planting. I've put some lettuce in. Now I want to sow some carrots. I want to sow me brussel sprouts and various other lots of cabbage. And I've got a few things in a small greenhouse which I've started off. They'll have to be taken up and potted and they're all due to go out as soon as the weather is kind enough.'

The moon rides high in the clear sky, promising fine days ahead. Bowder's Cottage sits warm and cosy on its small rise, one window winking back at the moon. Jack, in contemplative mood, was sitting by the fire. The strong, old head leant back against the worn cloth of the armchair. 'Can you tell me anything that wants to die? Animals, human beings, everything wants to live. Everything I've ever met wants to live, unless it's a nut case, whether it's been well-treated or ill-treated. This is why some poor people as have got terrible illnesses get over it. The want to live overrules the trouble. I mean, I've seen animals go through the most terrible things. When I was a young keeper there was an old man cutting some grass with two horses and a mowing machine. I was going up the hedge with me gun and he shouted to me, "Here. Come here young chap. I've just cut a hen pheasant. Look, I've cut her legs off and she's flown away into the wood". She'd left ten eggs there in the grass. So he pulled the horses on a bit and left a piece of grass uncut and covering the eggs. And I went along the next day when the old man had finished his job and I had a look, and the hen pheasant was back on the eggs. And I made a point of going and looking and I saw that pheasant for weeks and weeks, and she reared six young ones. And she only had the two stumps. And she went by the name of Stumpy. And she reared her little ones. It wants some doing that, but she managed it.'

If you asked Jack Lewis how he would like to be remembered, he would chuckle and the old face would screw up and the eyes twinkle, 'I *know* how I'll be remembered,' he would say, '. . . as a cantankerous, old bugger.' Let it be his epitaph for that extraordinary, old man would not have felt easy about his praises being sung.

FRENSHAM PONDS

FROM the Hog's Back in Surrey you can see some of the finest views in the south of England – though you risk your life on that frightening stretch of road if you become too enraptured. It is surprising how green and unpopulated the countryside seems, even though this is prime stockbroker belt and crowded by thrusting London commuters with their big, fast cars. On a fine spring or autumn morning the hills roll gently away into the distance and, with a little imagination and some cotton wool in your ears to block out the noise of the traffic, you can hear echoes of 'England's green and pleasant land'.

Even on a snowy February day, if you glance southwards from the Farnham end of the famous ridge, you can look out towards Frensham and its two renowned ponds. Frensham Great Pond is nearly two miles in circumference and was mentioned in 1208, when it was the property of the Bishop of Winchester. It provided his table at Farnham Castle with what must have been rather muddy-tasting fish, even though in 1749 Bowen's map recorded that Frensham had 'springs not inferior to those of Tunbridge Wells'. These springs created a pond, which was then enlarged, presumably so that still more fish could be caught and carried to the prelate's table. By 1913 it was large enough for the first seaplane to be tested on its placid waters.

Across nearby King's Ridge lies the Little Pond, beautiful in summer with water lilies, but often frozen enough for skaters in the winter months. Pine trees grow down to the edge of the water and ducks and coots swim amongst the graceful reeds along the banks. It dates back to 1246 and was also a notable provider of fish for the local churchmen. If eating fish is as good for the brain as it is supposed to be, they must have been a very bright bunch.

During the Second World War both ponds were drained to prevent them helping German pilots to find their targets in Aldershot and Bordon. On a moonlit night the surfaces would have reflected like mirrors to help the navigators plot their bombing runs. Local people can still remember catching stranded fish as the waters slipped away. History does not record whether they found anything more macabre than dying fish, for there have been many fatal drowning accidents in the deep, dark waters.

In the hot weather the area is thronged by visitors from London and the south — up for a day's swimming or boating or lazing in the sun. But in the depths of winter all life seems suspended and frozen into solemn silence. Yet even in the worst of the freeze much greenery remains. The poor, sandy soil makes a perfect platform for pine trees, holly and yew, which provide a permanent, dark green canopy in the area. At that time of the year you could easily imagine yourself in wildest Scotland or Wales, and it is impossible to believe that the glory that is London is less than an hour away.

THERE is certainly nothing frozen or lifeless about Peter Hoyte, whose shop is in the middle of Frensham village. A skilled and busy upholsterer and furniture-maker, he is also an avid collector. And his house is an Aladdin's cave of old sewing-machines, bicycles and musical boxes — to list only the beginning of his extraordinary collection. 'I came to Frensham as a boy. I used to visit Frensham Ponds and fell in love with the place. It's a good, tight, little village. It's true that there are quite a few stockbrokers and other outsiders here now. But there's a lot of the old brigade left too. Many of them have never moved. I've been here just fifteen years, but the majority of the people have lived here all their lives, and were born here.'

Peter has sharp, bright eyes behind his spectacles. He moves quickly and alertly between his shop and his upstairs workroom, where he once employed six people. Now he works on his own and sits amidst an artistic jumble of tools, machines and furniture as he builds and covers elegant chairs. Elsewhere, the walls and ceilings of his rooms are hung with the pieces he has collected over the years. In spring, summer and autumn he is besieged by visitors who come to admire his possessions, but the winter is quieter. 'Oh yes, it's good in the warm months. You can go for walks round the ponds, and this is a fantastic place to be then. It's full of visitors too, which is good for trade. But they come by in the winter as well sometimes to see my things. I started with sewing machines, 'cos they were allied to my job as an upholsterer. That was in the 1970s. Everybody started collecting then, 'cos they thought that it was all going to be lost for their children. And that's why I started. After sewing machines I got hooked on bicycles, and from bicycles I went on to mechanical music. Now it's anything that's worth having that turns up.'

Sometimes, for a treat, Peter Hoyte allows local children and their parents to ride his old bikes and tricycles in the narrow lanes around Frensham, where the river Wey carves its path through the Surrey meadows and flows under ancient bridges. The bicycles look well in keeping with the scene. 'The oldest bike I've got is an 1864 "bone-shaker" with metal wheels. That was the first bicycle with pedals and it gives you a bit of a bumpy ride. Before that it was the hobby-horse and people scooted along with their feet on the ground. That old bone-shaker was the first bike I ever bought, and soon afterwards I managed to get hold of a Penny-Farthing. Of course, old ladies and gentlemen couldn't ride them. They were too difficult. So they went on tricycles, which were invented a bit later.'

The melodious sounds of old, music hall tunes fill Peter's shop as he talks. The

Peter Hoyte in his workshop at Frensham. He is an avid collector of bicycles and music boxes as well as being a busy furniture maker and upholsterer.

grand, automatic music machines with their vast revolving drums and discs respond to the drop of an old penny. Here model horses race across the foreground. There a band of wooden monkeys clap their toy instruments in time to the beat. The quality of the sound is superb. The intricate machinery is a marvel of human ingenuity. The varnished woodwork gleams in the late afternoon light and from downstairs amongst the bicycles the tune of *Daisy Daisy* drifts upwards to clash with the monkey's rendition of *She was One of the Early Birds*. 'They're difficult to come by nowadays. There was a lot of stuff coming out of people's houses in the 1970s, and collectors were going for them then in a big way. But only museums have them now really. You don't find them locally or in antique shops. And, if they do come up in auctions, the bidding's pretty competitive, because you've got the Continentals, the Japanese and the Americans all after them. They're very lovely things and they're worth a few thousand quid too. But I don't think any have come up in sales for over nine years.'

As the music plays on, Peter adjusts his spectacles and turns back to tacking the seat of a smart chair for Portsmouth Corporation. His old curiosity shop surrounds him with history as he works at his cluttered bench.

THE wild and wooded heathland surrounding Frensham Ponds does not look after itself. It takes much work, skill and effort to keep it in trim and to protect plants, birds, deer and all the wildlife from the pressures of wind, weather and trippers. It is a full-time job for Ranger Stuart Dakers, who has the apparently impossible task of preserving the beauty of the countryside while catering for the recreation of thousands of tourists. 'It's a special place for all sorts of reasons, but mainly because of the need to reconcile the interests of conservation and recreation. It's a very delicate balance. Heathland is fragile as a habitat. But, because of the water, we're getting 300–500,000 people a year, all wanting to enjoy themselves, and their pleasure is frequently in conflict with the heathland itself. I don't blame them for coming here, because it can look glorious. The colours all complement each other – the browns, the greens and the yellows. And throughout the year, whether you've got the heather in bloom or lying low with the bracken coming through, and when you have the birches with the reddish tinge to their young branches in the early spring, the whole place is beautiful.'

Stuart joins a group of volunteers who are busily thinning out the young birches. Snow lies on the ground and a bonfire roars and crackles as it is fed with the new-cut wood. A tiny wren hops bravely backwards and forwards amongst the clumps of heather, keen to steal crumbs from the workers' lunch packs. 'The worst time for us is the spring. In the summer the visitors nearly all come for the water, and nobody much bothers to come out in the heathland. But in the spring, as soon as you get a good weekend, they pour out – dogs, kites and children – into the heather at the same time as the birds are nesting and everything else is mating. Then it can be very difficult. So what we have to do is quietly to persuade people to stick to the footpaths and not to throw sticks into the heather for their dogs, because there are birds nesting on the ground. On the whole I think we've got things under reasonable control and, which is crucial, people are enjoying the place.'

As Stuart and his team work their way up the hillside to the growl of their angry chain-saws, it is hard to imagine the summer hordes flocking through the place. In the frost and with the grey, winter sky it feels like the Russian steppes. 'The main problem with this heathland is that the heather needs constant light. The ground is just sand and acid with practically no nutrients. So, to survive, the heather needs light and the problem we have is the encroachment of birch, pine, gorse and bracken. The birch is a double problem. It shades the light out during the summer and, in the winter when it drops its leaves, it creates a sort of mulch on the ground and, if you look under the birch trees, you will see a mass of grass coming up. That spreads and the heather retreats before it. So our major function is to keep the heathland clear of birch and pine, and also to hold the bracken back. We can spray the bracken, but for birch and pine we have an annual pull and cut, which rotates round four major areas. So we come back to the start of the clearing cycle every four years.'

With his dog at his heels Stuart strides off up Stony Jump, from where he can look north towards the Hog's Back and south towards the Devil's Punch-Bowl. The Frensham heathland is spread out below him and he seems to be very much the master of all he surveys. Not far away to the east, fellow-ranger Duncan Mattinson is in charge of felling some mature pines in a patch of dense woodland. 'We're not in quite the same game as the commercial foresters. We're not just looking for the best trees. Sometimes we deliberately leave a dead tree or a rotten one for the woodpeckers. We might even decide to spare one because of an old crow's nest or a squirrel's drey, which hawks might like to use. So we're not pure foresters. We've got an emphasis on conservation in the way we manage the woodlands.'

The great trees crash to the ground amidst clouds of snow and dust and pine-needles. As the afternoon sky darkens, the flames from the woodmen's fire glitter through the trees, and the sound of the chain-saws doing their heavy labour echoes and reverberates among the nearby hills. 'This stand of Scots pines is between forty and sixty years old. It's never been looked after. It needs thinning. If we didn't thin it out the trees would become very tall. They wouldn't put on any more girth and they'd fall over in the wind. It's a bit like thinning carrots in a vegetable garden. You encourage the ones that remain and they grow thick and healthy. If you just left the trees and did nothing they would all grow thin and tall and be no use at all.'

As he moves round the areas of country for which he is responsible, Duncan is always on the look-out for the birds and animals, which make Frensham their home. 'We value the lizards and snakes, for they are very much a part of our heathland life. Then there are the run-of-the-mill birds you would expect in a place like this. In addition to them we have stonechats and wood-warblers, which are a little bit special. The biggest creatures up here are the roe-deer. On our thousand acres we have a population of about fifty. We do a census in April every year to give us an idea of what's about. Then, of course, there are masses of foxes. I'm afraid their numbers are artificially high because of the amount of litter brought in by the public and which the foxes feed on. There are plenty of rabbits, but no hares, because they don't like the sort of vegetation that grows here. And we have a wealth of smaller animals – mice and voles and that sort of thing, which provide food for kestrels and even for the occasional hobby or marsh harrier, although that's very rare indeed.'

Phil Roberts with his barge drawn by his horse *Domino* on the river Wey. In the summer months holiday makers can enjoy a trip up the river as their parents and grandparents would have travelled.

As dusk falls the work on the Scots pines continues and the long, straight trunks lie naked in the clearing as the fire consumes their branches. The frost returns and starts to freeze the already rock-hard ground.

AFTER the river Wey has run through Frensham it continues eastwards past smart houses and trim villages. A few miles further on it reaches Godalming where, on the old Wharf, Phil Roberts with the help of his trusty steed Domino, is getting into training for the summer months, when together they will pull holiday-makers up the river by barge, as they used to do it in the good, old days. The narrow-boat is long and lean and painted with bright, gypsy colours. The horse is piebald and strong, and the river is alive with ducks, geese, coots and moorhens. 'The big difference between pulling a barge and pulling a cart along a road is that the boat's in the middle of the river and the horse is on the tow-path. So he's having to pull at an angle instead of straight ahead. There's also a difference with the harness. We use cotton lines with rollers on instead of an upper trace. Or you can use chains with leather protectors. The point is to stop chafing because of the angle of the pull.'

The long-boat moves steadily downstream. The ice on the edges of the water rocks and cracks as the bow wave hits the bank. It is a venerable vessel, built in the Midlands in the mid-thirties for the Grand Union Canal Carrying Company. She spent most of her conventional working life trading between the Midlands and London. It was usually coal down to London and a mixture of cargoes like wheat and lime juice on the way back.

'When I got hold of her she'd been running horse-drawn boat trips on the Shropshire Union Canal since 1964. There aren't that many in the country now. There's a good one at Newbury on the Kennet and Avon Canal. Then there are two more in Devon, and you've got to go to the Midlands to find any more. I think there's only about half-a-dozen in the country.'

Domino strains at the long tow-rope, which cuts its way through the reeds along the river's edge. His heavy body leans outwards as it takes the weight and his big, hairy hooves scramble on the frozen mud of the tow-path. 'He's not a full shire. He's got a little bit of cob in him. So he isn't that big. But he's strong enough for the job. He has to give a helluva pull to get the thing started but, once it's moving, it's quite easy really. He came as a job lot with the boat. The only real problem we have had was when he fell into the river. That was because the tow-path had been undermined, and he trod right on the edge. But he was out under his own steam in a couple of minutes. He was rather wet and surprised, but not as surprised as walkers sometimes are when they come round the corner, choose the wrong side of the rope and then suddenly realise that they've got to duck or jump. Domino's unusual because he's done this work all his life. Most of the old boat-horses are former cart-horses, who've been on farms or were once "vanners". They're rather a scruffy collection of odds and sods. But he's done nothing else since he was a youngster.' Phil and Domino march on up towards Godalming lock, where the ice is thick and the houseboats line the banks. Man and horse must be fit because they have a long way to travel when the summer comes – about twenty miles a day and seven days a week.

SOUTHERN Surrey is hunting, shooting and fishing country, and there are plenty of people with the money to do all three. At Wishanger Stud at Churt Richard Twite can provide the facilities. He even has customers who are sufficiently enthusiastic to fish his stretch of the river Wey when the air temperature is freezing the line as it passes through the eyelets on the side of the rod. The river loops and bends. The snow is thick on the ground. And the lines hiss and whine as the experts cast their flies. 'It's a surprising area really. It's forty miles from London – less than an hour. And yet it's real country – very horsey with a lot of fishing and shooting and that type of thing. I was born in a small village about twenty miles away and I've been around here all my life. The Wey may not be in the same league as the Test and the Avon for fishing, but it's got a good character all the same. There's plenty of wild, brown trout and also a good head of grayling, known as the grey lady and a fine, fighting fish. Of course, there's a lot of coarse fish too in the river, but mainly it's trout and grayling.'

Richard is short and shaggy. His tweed hat is decorated with fishing flies. He smiles easily and his eyes move swiftly about him, taking in the detail of the

Progress has left hundreds of acres of heathland untouched in the area around Frensham Ponds. The two magnificent stretches of water once provided the fish for the Bishop of Winchester's table at Farnham Castle.

countryside. He fishes competently but without frills and, before long, he is landing a handsome rainbow trout. 'People come here from London and from Southampton and along the south coast – about a sixty mile radius. And we can teach them how to fish and shoot and to enjoy the country. It's not so much fun in the cold weather, but it certainly doesn't stop the fish biting. If the fishermen are keen enough to do it, then the fish are there for the taking. It's blowing a cold north-easterly today in this valley and it is a bit chilly, but we can stand it.'

The trees hang low over the water – a hazard for the unskilful. Hands and minds slow down in the freezing temperatures, but fish continue to be landed. 'There's no real season on rainbow. But there is on brown. If we catch brown trout in the river or in the lake between September and April we put them straight back. Trout fishing is my love. Shooting I enjoy. Both are here to be had and lots of people come to enjoy

Though in some areas of the country hedges are disappearing to suit modern farming methods, the ancient craft of hedge laying is still practised, as here in the Pevensey area, providing an attractive and completely stock-proof barrier.

Cowslips and violets are welcome harbingers of the springtime. In times past the sweet smell of violets was used to freshen the air of churches and homes after the long winter.

half a day's shooting and half a day's fishing. And then there's the wildlife. We've just spotted a heron taking a trout. We've got badger setts, and deer come out of the wood to drink at the lakeside. The whole place is swarming with animals and birds.'

In the afternoon, some of the fishermen join other enthusiasts to try their hand at clay-pigeon shooting. The black and orange discs fly and float from behind thick rhododendron bushes. The guns crack and crash and echo in the cold, bright air. The cries of 'pull' are closely followed by the zip and zing of the launchers. The marksmen, dressed in green and grey and khaki, are under the watchful eye of Bill Harding. 'What we're doing is teaching people to be safe, which is the main thing if you're using a firearm. Certainly, we're also teaching them to kill. But, at the same time, they're learning to use the gun comfortably, so that when they shoot at a live animal they kill it and don't just wound it. So safety is the main thing and, after that, it's gun mounting, position of the feet, position of the body in relation to the target you're shooting at and those sort of things. And it's not just to get ready to kill living creatures. Once people start clay shooting they will go on with it. It's a very popular sport in its own right, and it's becoming more so as the years go by. It's also much cheaper than shooting pheasants.'

There are some crack shots at Wishanger Stud. The clays explode in a cloud of black or orange powder. Some sail on through the air untouched and land with a thud in the undergrowth. High above, real pigeons sharply change course as they hear the fusillade from the ground. The clays rise from the bushes at different heights and at opposing angles. 'What we're doing is trying to simulate the flight of live birds. So each machine does a different job. One launches the clay, so that it's like a dropping pigeon coming in, and we would call that a decoying pigeon. Another ejects it like a driven partridge – fast and low. And another one throws it like a high pheasant. That gives variety to the sport and makes it challenging for the guns.'

As the gun-fire dies away, the men gather round a hot log fire outside the shooting hut to drink whiskey and to exchange stories. The boys with the clay-launchers arrive back from the wood and munch crisps and hamburgers. Peace settles back on the Surrey countryside. The winter moon rides high in a cloudless sky.

CLOSE to the Hog's Back in the little village of Compton, painter Mary Wondrausch works as one of the leading slipware artists in the country. This ancient pottery craft takes intense concentration, a steady hand and infinite patience. Mary's home is old and splendidly eccentric, full of colour and warmth. The beams are hung with garlic and herbs. Chunky pottery bowls and plates are everywhere. And the walls of the rooms are hand-painted by Mary with flowers and colourful patterns. The little house sits at the end of a rough track and is guarded by a donkey, some hens and a cat called Lotus Feet.

'I started off in the town, and it made an amazing difference when I moved to the country. Before that, I didn't think that I was inspired by nature. But I found wonderful light here. And the chickens appear in the pottery, and the cat and the

Mary Wondrausch demonstrating the ancient pottery skill of slipware, at which she is a leading exponent, at her studio in Compton.

donkey. The trees and flowers too. It's altered my work considerably. For instance, I find that I'm drawing birds much more on the plates, although that kind of thing isn't in the English tradition, which dates back to the 17th century. The potters in those days weren't using the natural things that happened in the world around them. They weren't drawing on nature at all. All the work came from symbols – kings and queens, Adam and Eve, the Prince of Wales's feathers.'

Mary throws a pot with practised fingers on her wheel and then moves down the studio to the place where the hardest part of her work is done. She picks up a large and perfectly rounded plate, pours beige liquid into it with a steady hand and swirls it slowly round and round until the whole surface is covered. 'It's called slipware because this clay solution is "the slip". It has that name because it just slips about on the plate. So this is a particular type of pottery which is made in red clay and has this solution of slip poured over it. And it's always decorated when it's wet.'

There is some faint recollection of a master baker at work on a royal wedding cake as Mary squeezes more wet clay through a home-made tube and produces pictures, faces and patterns on the damp surface of the plate. In the last three centuries artists used a cow's horn or a clay vessel to produce the picture, but Mary's device means that she can work more accurately and have greater control. 'I came to do this because it's so difficult. Most other potters seem to do stoneware. But I used to spend a lot of time abroad in Spain and in France and I just loved the ordinary, peasant pottery. And I couldn't find anybody who knew how to do it, so there was nobody to teach me. I was determined to have a go, even though it was very hard. And the most wonderful thing about slipware is that you can use words on the plates. I can make pots and plates that convey sentiment. I make special plates for people to commemorate their marriage or the birth of a child, and I love that relationship with the people. It's a continuing relationship too because I've been able to do wedding plates and then plates for the children of that marriage.'

Bulls are definitely discouraged from coming into Mary Wondrausch's pottery shop, but that does not mean that there are not occasional mishaps. 'One day I was showing a group of nice children how to do the "slipping" on a big plate. I was being terribly clever and flinging it around in my hands and I dropped the whole thing into the barrel of slip. There was a great splash and all the children were smothered. And they'd all come wearing their best clothes, so I wasn't very popular.'

THE area around Frensham Ponds is a place of contrasts. It is true that London is just up the road. It is true that many of the posh houses look hostile and unwelcoming with their burglar alarms and luxury limousines. It is true that rush hour traffic streams through the district. And yet, what the optimists call progress has left untouched hundreds of acres of priceless heathland and, in the winter months at least, the two magnificent stretches of water. Perhaps, like God, nature is not easily mocked, and she seems to have a way of repelling even the most determined invasions of urban man.

PEVENSEY LEVELS

IN 1066 William the Conqueror brought the Norman fleet to Pevensey and landed unopposed. This part of the seashore, half-way between Bexhill and Eastbourne, is still known as Norman's Bay, and the region behind it is flat and bleak and marshy. It is called Pevensey Levels, and it is as ancient and as full of atmosphere as the Romney Marsh – a few miles to the east. There was a fine Roman castle at Pevensey, and the Normans built their own mighty stronghold on its site. It is still a magic place with fine, old, battered walls enclosing a broad stretch of springy grass. The traffic circling the fortifications might be a million miles away and, when the mists lie low over the dykes and the sheep and cattle loom out of the murk, it is possible to forget the twentieth century and to imagine what it was like here a thousand years ago.

When the Romans were at Pevensey, which they called Andrieda, it was a deep sea bay dotted with small islands. Over the years it became the largest area of Sussex enclosed by sea dykes. By the 8th century the tides had dragged enough shingle along the coast to protect the saltmarsh from the sea, which sometimes spilled over these natural barriers. During the 12th and early 13th centuries the Levels changed from marshland to water-meadows and finally to arable fields. In the Domesday Book an amazing 294 saltworks are mentioned in the area, for in mediaeval times it became famous for salt-making as the summer workers pursued the sea-water and held it back with trenches and temporary dykes, waiting for the sun to evaporate it and to give them their precious harvest. Today it is beef, corn and lamb country and a place for summer holidays. But enough of the mystery of the old marsh remains to give it a feeling of adventure and romance. And for bird watchers there are waders galore, owls, harriers, geese, ducks, swans and gulls and the opportunity, over the flatlands, to see them easily and from far off.

When fog is forecast you can be fairly sure to find it on the Pevensey Levels. Here there is the scent of smuggling and the tang of twilight. In the heart of the marshland it is possible to imagine that the inhabitants in the distant past would recognise much of it today with the pylons made invisible and the sound of traffic muffled by the gloom. In those old, far-off days everyone had to rely on his neighbour to keep the ditches and streams, which passed through all the land, clear and running, so that the marshes could be drained. This feeling of reliance remains today, and the people seem private and self-contained with strangers.

Hares and rabbits have been hunted and killed on the Pevensey Levels for centuries, and have been an important part of the diet of working people for whom more conventional meat may have been too expensive. For cousins Colin and Dennis Huggett from Westham, rabbit is as valuable a source of food as ever it was, and they and their ferrets are out on the prowl whenever time allows. Colin has a pleasant face and eyes that smile even in the coldest weather. 'I'm a marsh man through and through. Born here. Bred here. There's no other place like it, even though it's changed quite a bit. A lot of the hedgerows are gone. A lot of the ponds are being filled in. And we're losing a fair bit of wildlife. Moorhens are going and we've got a lot of mink, which we never had before. They're quite destructive. We've found them in rabbit burrows, and that means they've got to the rabbits before we have.'

Colin and Dennis walk through the winter vegetables to the bottom of the garden, where the ferrets are kept in two small hutches. They scrabble at the woodwork and the wire netting as they hear the footsteps approaching. The long, thin creatures are handled and talked to gently before being lowered carefully into a carrying box. The two cousins set off into the early morning mist – figures out of a Victorian novel. 'Most of the Pevensey farmers have been driven to change. They were told to grow more corn, so they've ploughed up the marginal land, which would never have had corn on it in the past. As more corn is grown, more land is ploughed and more is reclaimed. Some of the marshes have been drained, so a lot of the ducks and wildfowl that used to be there have gone. It used to flood from November right through to March, but the river authorities have put in pumps and lowered the water table for the corn. Where it used to be rushes and cattle-grazing it's wheat and barley. It's nice to see corn growing, of course, but it doesn't replace the hares and the otters that used to be here. They've gone. But the marshes themselves are just about hanging on. It's wild here in the winter – a bit of an inhospitable place out in the rain and wind. But it's still sad to see so much of it go. If you're here in the spring, when the blackthorn and hawthorn are out and in blossom, it's a wonderful place.'

The men arrive at an old pond in a meadow, where the brambles and rushes have been cleared by hand to reveal a score of burrows. Fresh droppings and newly turned soil are everywhere. The Pevensey Levels stretch away into the fog. In the distance a stone-mason chips at a chimney-stack and the sounds of hammer on stone drift through the murk. Colin and Dennis busily start to peg purse-nets over the holes. The ferrets move restlessly in their box. 'When you think that the rabbit population was as good as wiped out by myxomatosis and only 1% was left, they've come back very well. Well for us, that is. Not very well for the farmers, 'cos they still don't like 'em. But rabbits go pretty well anywhere – even close up to houses. We don't ferret near houses. We usually use these small purse-nets but, sometimes at night, we use a long net round the whole warren, because it's easy to lose rabbits in the dark if you're not careful.'

As the ferrets are lowered into the holes Colin and Dennis keep very still and press

Dennis Huggett, a marshman born and bred, pictured here with one of his ferrets.

their heads to the ground listening for the sounds of rabbits on the move. Soon there is action as brown and grey bundles of fur leap out into the waiting nets, and there is a lot of dashing backwards and forwards, and cries of, "Rabbit up!". Every now and again a small, inquisitive ferret's face peeps out of a burrow and then turns and disappears again. 'When there was a lot of rabbits we could keep some for the pot and hand some out to other people in the village, and sell the rest. But we don't get that many now – not in the vast quantities we had before myxomatosis. But you can still sell them. They're worth £1 a pound now. There used to be a market for their skins. The rag and bone man used to come, so it was good business. You got two shillings and sixpence for a rabbit and one and threepence for the skin, which was very good. But there's no trade for them now, so you just give them away. But the meat is lovely.'

Nearly a score of freshly killed rabbits hang from a walking stick by their hind legs. The men gather up their nets and talk kindly to the ferrets as they put them back in their boxes. The two men stride off into the mist, and peace descends upon the marshland meadow until the next time.

NOT far to the north of the marshes stands magnificent Michelham Priory, which was founded in 1229 by the Norman Lord of Pevensey. The name Michelham means 'the hamlet in the bend of the river'. The stream in question is the Cuckmere and its waters drive the wheel of a watermill, which is first mentioned in 1434 but probably goes back much further, since Thomas a Becket is said to have fallen into the millpool at Michelham when out hunting.

The hard-working miller is Gilbert Catt, who lives in a house called Millstones on Mill Road in nearby Hailsham. He is a small, frail old man, but there are undercurrents of great strength in his character, and milling is in his family's blood for generations. 'If you come to this place when the sun shines you get a show of rural England that we see so little of these days. This mill was shut down and out of action for fifty years and I never expected to see it running again. Then one day someone told me it had been restored, so I went to see what was happening. And sure enough the mill was there making a start. In the fifty years out of use most of the machinery had gone. There was no wheel and hardly any mechanical pieces. Probably what happened was that any ironwork went out during the last war to help the war effort. So that left very little behind – just some of the wood really. They virtually had to start from scratch.'

As the old man cranks open the water gate, the heavy wheel slowly begins to thump and churn. The water bubbles and boils and, as the great cylinder gets up speed, the sound it makes is full of music and as old as history. 'We were millers and corn-merchants at Hailsham. My grandfather came to Hamlins Mill in Mill Road a hundred years ago. He took over the mill in 1886 until he died. Then my father took it on until he died and, when my brother died in 1967, I couldn't carry on any longer on me own. He died in the January and I ran to the end of the following September. Then I had to close down. Our mill was a windmill of course, built in 1834 and destroyed by fire in 1923, when my parents built what they called a steam-mill.'

Gilbert Catt moves across to the mighty, horizontal wooden wheel inside the mill at Michelham and throws it into gear, linking it to the vertical water-wheel outside. As the machinery begins to turn the whole building trembles with the weight of its moving burden. High above more wheels are turning and the great mill-stones begin to revolve and grind the wheat.

Fine flour pours into bags powdering Gilbert Catt's face and eyebrows with white dust. In the apex of the mill's roof an ancient wooden wheel, geared by the tug of a rope, lifts heavy sacks of corn up to the bins. A flight of Canada geese arrives noisily on the lake beside the mill-pond. The miller, eyes alert, moves busily back and forth, checking the fineness of the flour and watching the old machinery constantly as it groans and strains and grumbles.

'You've got to keep an eye on it all the time, particularly the mill-stones. You can't run away and leave them. With most other types of grinder – the modern ones – you can set it up and leave it. But not mill-stones. They're quite different. They're very temperamental. You've got to watch them all the time to see that the settings are where you want them. As you feel the flour coming down the spout you can tell whether it's too fine or too coarse or coming down too fast or too slow, and you make the necessary adjustments as you go along. It's very largely a matter of experience. After a number of years you get the feel of the flour – whether it's just right or just what you want. And it's only by experience that you can get there. You can't pick on anyone and ask them to be a miller. The learning and experience are necessary.'

The small, bent figure turns back to his work. His physique is a complete contrast to the heavy machinery which surrounds him and which he controls. Outside, the mill-race tumbles and turns as it falls towards the Cuckmere. Snowdrops are out beside the water, and the first daffodils and primroses are beginning to show.

ALL along the south coast fishing seems to produce a breed of strong and independent men, whose values owe nothing to modern fads and fashions. The boats they sail differ in shape and style, depending on the type of beach they live on. But their attitudes and actions are firm and determined. John Gell and his wife live on the sea-front at Pevensey Bay. Often he fishes alone from his stubby, strong boat while she looks after their popular fish shop.

'I've been on this beach all my life since I was born in 1937. I started as a fisherman with my father as a boy, and then, when I left school at fifteen, I took it over and carried on from then, which is now thirty-four years. When we get the east to south-east or southerly winds up to gale 9 or 10, the sea can come right over the top and flood us out. We actually had it nearly four feet deep in our bungalow about twenty years ago. When the weather's like that we pull the boat down to the side of the house for shelter.'

John is a large, ruddy-faced man, dressed in yellow waterproofs. His hands are big and cracked from the wind and salt water. His boat stands high on the shingle, surrounded by nets and fish boxes and the debris of a fisherman's life. As he carries heavily-greased wooden planks down the beach to make a path to the sea for the boat, his wife stands by on a winch beside their house to release the metal cable which is used to take the strain when the boat sets out or to pull it up the shingle when it returns.

'If you have a good slope on the beach it slides down very well. But if we get a lot

Three generations of Gilbert Catt's family have been millers at Hailsham. Today he operates this restored watermill on the river Cuckmere which still produces stone ground flour, just as it did centuries ago.

of easterly wind it causes banks, and then we have to plough them and shovel them to get the boat down because it's too heavy to push over them.'

The boat reaches the incoming tide and John Gell jumps aboard and heads out to sea. His nets have been left out overnight and he is hoping for a good catch to satisfy the customers, who will soon be queueing up at the shop. There is a tiny cabin in the stern of the boat – the size of an allotment tool-shed. But almost all the work has to be done out in the wind and weather. 'During the summer months here night-trawling we used to get a tremendous amount of Dover sole. But there's hardly any at all now. Same in the spring for plaice. We used to get lots. But it's gradually all being over-fished by foreigners and by our own fishermen as well. We're getting too clever at catching fish, and we're catching them faster than they can breed. Back about twenty-five years ago I was the only fisherman in the Bay. There was an odd boat here and there, but it's in the last ten years that it's really come on. In the old days it was just done by my grandfather, who handed it down to my father and then to me.'

But in those days it was not just fishing that brought boats to the Pevensey shore, because this was a notorious smuggling coast. 'My grandfather had a biggish, old sailing boat, similar to mine but larger – no motor in it – and they used to do the smuggling with lobster pots about five mile out. The Frenchmen would put the brandy in the pots and he'd pull them in and bring it back with the fish. Of course, my grandfather used to own the old Castle Inn in Pevensey Bay, so the stuff came in handy for him. They used to get up to quite a caper, especially with the excise men all over the place. I think he must have been pretty crafty.'

Soon John is pulling a fair catch of plaice over the side of his boat. After a couple of hours he turns and heads for home. 'Over the years I've got used to fishing alone. The hardest part is getting the boat down the beach, because you have to push it down on the oak skids and you can damage your back if you're not careful. On the way home it's all right because the winch does the work.' So even tough Sussex fishermen are afflicted by back trouble, one of the scourges of the sedentary, late-twentieth century. Some small consolation, perhaps, for the city office-workers, who think of a fisherman's life with longing on those slow, hot London afternoons.

MEN have been making trugs in Sussex for over two hundred years. The strong and beautifully-shaped baskets can be found all over the world. Yet most of them are made in Herstmonceux on the high ground to the north of Pevensey Levels. Here David Sherwood and his team apply the skills which have been passed down over many generations. One of his trusted craftsmen is Raymond Smith. 'My family goes back to the early 18th century in these parts, and I've been involved in trug-making for over forty years. It's all done by eye, this job. You've got to have a good sense of balance and of proportion. If you haven't got a good eye you get a trug with a handle that's crooked and, when you go to put the first board in, the trug can look off-centre.'

Just down the road from the truggery, stacks of wood stand like wigwams in a grass meadow. Young men saw and split the logs by hand and with easy precision. 'We use sweet chestnut for the framework and willow for the boards to go in the cradle. The chestnut comes in various lengths from the woodsmen, and it's broken in half and then quartered again. Then the centres are taken out and they're shaved to the widths and thickness we need. Then they're stood back for a little while to dry out – just a little bit, and from then on it's a matter of putting them in a steamer for about ten minutes, shaping them round a former, starting with the handle. Next you make the framework and the handle's got to be ready to slip over that to hold it all together and to save it from bowing out.'

74

Three men sit in a row on old benches working at the baskets. Wood shavings surround them. The tools of their trade – knives, hammers and bradawls – are close at hand. They speak seldom, because it is a job which demands concentration. The sweet smell of new wood fills the air. 'Most of our willow comes from the Home Counties. I'm sorry to say that we have culled out quite a lot of it now, and the farmers there are not in the habit of replanting where the trees were cut down. I think they should do, because it's generally grown in a piece of ground where nothing else will grow, but with plenty of water.

'It only needs fifteen feet apart each way for one of these maiden trees to grow. It's a ten year policy and they could have a nice little income from it. A lot of the wood we get comes from the off-cuts from cricket bat people. It's wonderful wood. It's long grain and lends itself to bending and looks nice and white. But the trees we cut down are getting few and far between. We've got to go further away and then you get costings coming into it.'

Raymond reacts angrily to the idea that his is a dying industry. 'Oh no! Along the line, somebody has said that it's a disappearing craft. Well, it isn't. Far from it. People who come and buy trugs must see the potential. My guv'nor has employed new people recently and quite successfully too. We've got one lad here at twenty-five. He's a sawyer. And we've got another chap – he's a little older than that – and he's got quite a confident manner with his cleaving action and doing the steaming and all to do with the chestnut. He'll graduate from that into boards and then produce trugs at the end of it. The length of the apprenticeship depends on the individual. I mean, if the person's as thick as two planks put together, it takes longer to sink in. But for anybody with a little bit of common sense it doesn't take all that time. What shall I say? A couple of years before you can sit down and say that it really looks like a trug.'

Stacks of finished baskets stand at the side of the shed. Outside, others hang from the door-posts to tempt passing motorists. And in gardens a thousand miles away you will find them stalwartly serving the same purpose that they have served for centuries.

THE chief inhabitants of the marshes used to be sheep and cattle and the lookers, who were responsible for looking after the sheep of the absentee landlords. Today the lookers are no more, but there are still marvellous shepherds around and they have trained their dogs with uncanny precision. One of them is Roy Standen from Boreham Street, whose four black and white collies are as obedient and disciplined as guardsmen outside Buckingham Palace.

'This is a wonderful, remote place. It's wild in the wintertime. It's very good in the summer. It's always cooler down here. It's fine sheep country, though a lot of it has been ploughed up now for growing corn. During the war we tried to grow corn down here without any draining. But since the war they've drained it and they're growing corn very successfully because the ground is so strong, never having been cultivated before. It was so fertile and the corn grew so well that some of the binders – this was before combines – couldn't cope with it.

'There were quite a number of lookers here in the old days. But now most of the people drive round in a Land Rover and look themselves. But when I first came down here there was a family of Fields – two boys and a father – and they used to do the looking right through the Pevensey marshes. And then there was Bob Pope and his sons. They did a lot of looking. But Bob died about a fortnight ago. So there's not many left now.'

Roy's dogs fall into line at his heels as he lets them out of their individual kennels. Down on the marsh he sends them off to round up a herd of sheep in a big field surrounded by dykes. At long range his quiet commands are obeyed to the letter. And even if two of the dogs look reluctant to sit still on guard while the others run and round up the sheep, they do not move a muscle until their master whispers the word. 'They're very keen to work these dogs. Their hearing is sharp. If a dog is sluggish it doesn't work as quickly or as neatly. But these ones, you've only got to give them half a command and they go – sometimes before you want them to. I think the thing is that if you work them quietly normally, then, if they do something wrong and you shout at them, it frightens them and they stop straight away. They've all got names. You say the name first. I've got the same commands for all four, but if you say the name first, then the command, they'll take it.'

The sheep are quickly rounded up and are headed into a pen. In the rush one of them is jostled into a dyke. Its heavy fleece, weighed down by water, makes it impossible for it to escape without assistance. For once the dogs are helpless. They stand and watch anxiously as Roy rescues the drowning ewe.

'The dogs vary a lot. Mr Wallace, who was one of the finest sheepdog-handlers ever known, reckoned that they had to be two years old before you could really trust them outside. If you take seven years of our lives to one of a dog's, that makes the dog about fourteen and that's when he reckons it's time for them to start work. I train them one at a time – never together. They get into bad habits if you have another dog with them. They'll either cut in to get there first, or I've occasionally had a dog that won't go unless another dog's with it. It looks for another dog before it'll go itself. So I always do one at a time. Breeding's important with this job too. But, like with humans, it doesn't always work. You know, you can put a good bitch to a good dog, but you don't always get good puppies.' As Roy works through the flock, trimming their feet and checking their legs, the eager faces of the four dogs peer through the railing, begging for more action and more work.

IN Peelings Lane, Pevensey there is an old smithy, which dates back to the last century. Here Sam Fanaroff works wonders in copper, silver, pewter and brass. Three of England's greatest artists – Turner, Constable and Samuel Palmer – came to paint the Pevensey marshes in all their delicate moods. Sam also draws his inspiration from the Levels. 'When I came to Pevensey from South Africa I had a

Though more and more reclaimed marshland on the Pevensey Levels is being turned over to the plough, there are many stretches of pasture left for the traditional sheep and cattle farming of this area.

strange experience. The first time I saw the castle I knew I'd seen it before, though I'd never even heard of it. Years later a spiritualist told me that I'd lived at Pevensey in the 11th century. This was surprising but it did fit in with various images that I've always carried throughout my life but never managed to explain. So all those things seemed to come together like a jigsaw puzzle and it means that I feel part of this place. The village has a sense of community and people have a sense of belonging to it because it has a heart. There's the castle and the church and we still have a school. And there's a grocer and a butcher and a baker and a newsagent, and people see each other every day. And there is a feeling that they belong and that people care. So it's rather nice, and I hope it continues and isn't spoilt.'

Sam's workshop is an extraordinary jumble of metal and tools and works of art. A tough twist of ivy has fought its way under the roof and has climbed down towards the old heater. The warmth has made the plant pale and brittle. Sam heats metal until it glows with a blow torch and then attacks it with one of his heavy hammers.

'I've been a craftsman for thirty years, and the good thing about being a craftsman is that you're making things which people want or need. And there's an added bonus that, when I'm dead and gone, somebody's going to say "Well, I wonder who made that". And that'll be me of course, and I'll be looking up or down, whichever it may be and saying, "Yes, it's me that made it". And there won't be another object quite the same anywhere. I think that's the whole essence of individual craftsmanship. It's unique in every sense, unlike mass production. That's the reason craftsmen survive, because they are producing things of individual character.'

Beside the village pond across the road from the smithy the sound of metal under pressure drifts across the black surface of the water, but fails to disturb the ducks and the geese as they enjoy the early spring sunshine. They have heard it all before.

NOWHERE in Sussex has changed so much and so often as Pevensey Levels. The marshmen in the Middle Ages fought against the invading sea with dykes, sluices, tide gates and water-lets. Sometimes they won. Sometimes they lost. And depending on their success, the marshes changed. But in success or failure men have always loved the marshland – and Rudyard Kipling was one of them:

> 'I'm just in love with all these three,
> The Weald and the Marsh and the Down countree.
> Nor I don't know which I love the most
> The Weald or the Marsh or the white chalk coast.
>
> I've buried my heart in a ferny hill,
> Twix a liddle low shaw an' a great high gill.
> Oh, hop-line yaller an' wood-smoke blue,
> I reckon you'll keep her middling true.
>
> I've loosed my mind for to out and run
> On a Marsh that was old when kings begun.
> Oh, Romney Level and Brenzett reeds
> I reckon you know what my mind needs.
>
> I've given my soul to the Southdown grass,
> And sheep-bells tinkled where you pass.
> Oh, Firle an' Ditchling an' sails at sea,
> I reckon you keep my soul for me.'

INDEX

Baker, Graham 23, 24
Beachy Head 22
Billingham, Mark 32
Boreham Street 75

Catt, Gilbert 71
Churt 61
Cole, Wally 44
Coleman, Jack 20
Compton 65
Cook, Bill 43
Copper, Bob 22
Crowborough, Warren 11

Dakers, Stuart 58

Etchingham 29

Fanaroff, Sam 76
Farnham Castle 55
Fords Green 17

Gascoigne, John 24
Gell, John 72, 73
Glynde 23
Godalming 60

Hailsham 71
Hall, Di 25
Hall, Peter 25
Harding, Bill 65
Harding, Marion 29

Haremere Hall 29
Harrison, Don 12, 13
Herstmonceux 74
Hogs Back 55
Howe, Christine 12
Hoyte, Peter 56
Huggett, Colin 69
Huggett, Dennis 69

King's Ridge 55
Kirby, Fred 17

Lavis, John 29
Lawrence, Dave 37
Lawrence, Jamie 32, 33
Lewis, Jack 48–54
Lewis, John 51
Lintock, Keith 34
Lord, Bob 37, 38

Mattinson, Duncan 59
Michelham Priory 71

Nutley 11, 14

Osbourne, Nigel 34

Pagham 37
Paine, Michael 40, 41
Phillips, Harry 42
Pope, Bob 76

Ringmer 20
River Brede 39
River Cuckmere 71
River Medway 11
River Ouse 11
River Tillingham 39
River Wey 60
Roberts, Phil 60
Rodmell 25
Rottingdean 22

Severn Sisters Country Park 24
Sheffield Park 12
Sherwood, David 74
Smith, Raymond 74
Standen, Ray 75

Steyning 22
Stony Jump 59

Twite, Richard 61

Uckfield 12
Upfold, George 35, 36

Webb, Alan 44, 47
Westham 69
Wilcock, Margaret 12
Wilcock, Marion 12, 14, 15
Wilcock, Paul 14, 15
Williams, Sian 14
Wondrausch, Mary 65, 67
Wych Cross 12, 14